Alice Thomas Ellis

was born in Liverpool and educated at Bangor Grammar School and Liverpool School of Art. She is the author of ten widely praised novels, *The Sin Eater*, *The Birds of the Air*, *The 27th Kingdom*, *The Other Side of the Fire*, *Unexplained Laughter*, *The Skeleton in the Cupboard*, *The Clothes in the Wardrobe* and *The Fly in the Ointment*, and two studies of juvenile delinquency, *Secrets of Strangers* and *The Loss of the Good Authority*, written with psychiatrist Tom Pitt-Aikens. From 1985 to 1989 she wrote a weekly column in the *Spectator* under the title 'Home Life', which gained her a readership even wider than her novels and which was published in four highly acclaimed volumes by Flamingo. *Cat Among the Pigeons* is a collection of her pieces published in the *Catholic Herald*, for which she started writing a regular column in 1992. She lives in ⋯⋯⋯⋯ Wales with her husband ⋯⋯⋯⋯

ALICE THOMAS ELLIS

Cat Among the Pigeons

A Catholic Miscellany

Flamingo
An Imprint of HarperCollinsPublishers

f l a m i n g o	The term 'Original' signifies publication direct into paperback with no preceding British hardback edition.
O RIGINAL	The Flamingo Original series publishes fine writing at an affordable price at the point of first publication.

Flamingo
An Imprint of HarperCollins*Publishers*
77–85 Fulham Palace Road,
Hammersmith, London W6 8JB

First published in Great Britain by Flamingo 1994
9 8 7 6 5 4 3 2 1

Copyright © Alice Thomas Ellis 1994

The text of this book appeared originally
as articles in the *Catholic Herald*

The Author asserts the moral right to
be identified as the author of this work

Author photograph by Jerry Bauer

A catalogue record for this book
is available from the British Library

ISBN 0 00 654818 0

Set in Baskerville

Printed in Great Britain by
HarperCollinsManufacturing Glasgow

Contents

Contents

A Thankless Task

'Well shiver my timbers,' I remarked moderately, finishing off my half of bitter. I had just read a passage including me, albeit tongue-in-cheek, among the 'revered guardians of the nation's conscience'. Things have come to a pretty pass, reflected I, if they have to dig so deep in the barrel. Other names mentioned were those of certain Anglican clerics who I wouldn't trust to guard the cat's meat, so I was quite secure from falling into the sin of pride. Squeaks of mirth from family and friends further protected me from this failing. Besides, guardians of the nation's conscience are frequently equated with prophets of doom, and while I see their point I get the impression they usually have a tough time.

Cassandra, Jeremiah, Savonarola, Chicken Licken, Mary Whitehouse and the man with the sandwich board proclaiming THE END IS NIGH all have not endeared themselves to their fellows.

Where, I wondered – getting annoyed now – are the professionals whose *job* it is to guard the nation's conscience? Mostly behind the parapet, is where: with their heads well down. Many seeming not merely to lack the courage of their convictions but to lack all conviction. It is possible to picture them ambling about the Cities of the Plain intoning 'we are all guilty', terrified of appearing illiberal except of course

1

when it comes to smoking (anti) and feminism (pro) since here they are backed to the hilt by the politically correct. On other questions of manners, morals and doctrine they mostly dither about like so many hens.

How reassuring then to learn that the Pope has had the excellent good sense to require Matthew Fox to pipe down. I heard this person (Matthew Fox, that is) bleating on the radio the other morning that his dismissal was an act of 'institutionalized violence' and putting in a plea for his 'Creation Spirituality'. In his work *The Coming of the Cosmic Christ* we find: 'The idea of a private salvation is utterly obsolete . . . the cosmic Christ can be both female and male, heterosexual and homosexual . . . I believe there is a need to recover the sense of both lust and chastity as powers and therefore virtues within all people . . .' I don't know what he thinks he means by this, but unless I'm much mistaken there appears to be a whiff of heresy here. I am told that in his Institute for Culture and Creation Spirituality in California (natch) he employed a witch known as Starhawk, who is keen on sacking God and installing Goddess in His place, a process known, I believe, as reverse discrimination but surely not one to invite the approval of the Vatican. These people are doubtless entitled to their own opinions but it is expecting too much to ask that the Pope should agree with them. It is now fashionable in certain circles to deplore the views and influence of the Pope, to describe him as 'a terrible, terrible man' as Karen Armstrong did in an interview in the *Evening Standard*. This is doubtless because he still sees it as his role to guard the conscience of the nations. A thankless task and one I do not envy him. Satan and wicked spirits are still wandering the world intent on the ruin of souls, and as long as there are those who persist in regarding him and his friends as an oppressed minority we need people in authority to argue

2

against the trend. I don't mind doing my bit but I've also got the housework to do and anyway I'm going back to bed now. God bless the Pope.

Good News

I thought I'd begin today on a note of cheer. By temperament I incline to the pessimistic: that is, I do not fall upon the post with eager anticipation. I circle it warily, suspecting it will consist of communications from the taxman or requests that I appear on live television, or send money to save the hedgehog. Nor do I leap to answer the telephone. It's bound to be the taxman or someone else whose letter I have not answered. I do not go happily to parties expecting to meet someone interesting and I do not like it when the doorbell rings. I hope for the best but have a regrettable tendency to expect the worst.

You'll be wondering where the cheer comes in, so I'll tell you. Earlier this year our youngest son went off with his girlfriend to explore Africa. While they were away I heard little but horror stories about the place: famine and tragedy, civil war and crime. Tourists were done to death in game parks or robbed by bandits in their hotels. The overall impression was of a dark continent suffused by gloom. I scarcely expected ever to see them again. In the course of time they returned (this is where the cheer begins) and I was pleasantly surprised to find that they had not contracted the new incurable strain of malaria, had not been bitten by rabid animals (now I come to think of it, the top-up rabies vaccine

4

is still sitting in the fridge) nor attacked by robbers. They had had a perfectly delightful time watching well-disposed wild beasts and had met with nothing from humankind but kindness and courtesy. The food had left something to be desired, but then it always does on tourist routes. Fast or Expensive were the alternatives. The Fast was all fried, as in one egg, tomato and chips; chips, tomato and two eggs; tomato, chips, beans and an egg etc., or toasted sandwiches. On one occasion when the choice lay between cheese and tomato, or onion and cheese the travellers requested cheese, tomato *and* onion all together in one sandwich, and the restaurant came to a standstill as the staff spent half an hour debating the feasibility of such a recherché combination. I have had the same experience in motorway cafés in Britain but you expect foreigners to be more flexible. They were in the end when the niceties of the situation were ironed out. Why – I asked – did you not eat cassava root? The travellers said they had not been offered any but had tried cooked flying ants and they were most acceptable. Not all that different from shrimp, I suppose: just a land-locked delicacy of rather similar appearance. Now the travellers are home their post – apart from the usual despondency-laden buff envelopes – is charming and invigorating. They receive letters from people they met on their journeyings, full of affection and good will. One dear child is anxious to know how their harvesting went and whether they have gathered in all the crops. She writes, 'I hope you liked your stay in Uganda, especially at Hotel Gloria, but most I hope you had the best time in the peace of Africa.'

I was reflecting on this when a new lot of post arrived. It included a card from my Xhosa friend Lillian, who is working as a counsellor and psychotherapist with a group of students in a Cathar district near the Pyrenees. She says, 'It's a medieval place, dating far back, full of history, treachery, intrigue, violence, romanticism and pathos – could be the twentieth century too, I suppose.' This timely reminder of Europe's violent and unadmirable past caused me to wonder how I would have felt had I been a medieval parent and the children had elected to visit Cathar country. Not too cheerful, I imagine. However, they would doubtless have met some kindly and good people even then. Now the quality of the post is improving I'm going to read letters instead of newspapers. Sometimes they actually contain Good News.

A Spoonful of Sugar

I read somewhere the other day or someone told me or I heard it on the radio (I don't think I imagined it) that stress is good for you. It sends the adrenalin coursing through the system like carbolic acid down the drains. I may not have got that quite right but it is another cheering thought. It is also a further example of received wisdom standing on its head. Until five minutes or so ago stress was supposed to be bad for you. In a Victorian book on feminine loveliness and how to achieve it the author states categorically that the reason Turkish women had such glowing complexions and perfect teeth was that they ate copious amounts of sugar. We have recently learned that cholesterol is no longer the monstrous substance it was once considered but is now perceived as necessary, albeit in modest amounts, to prevent us from committing suicide or spending our days sunk in Siberian gloom. I am not aware of the precise status of salt at the moment but for a time it was abhorred by the health conscious, thus rendering their cooking inedible. I had always believed it was essential to the vital processes, especially if you worked hard and sweated a lot. Labourers, it was said, added it to their beer in order to top up the saline levels thus, I would imagine, rendering it undrinkable. A judicious intake of red wine is now said to be beneficial whereas once there were those who regarded all alcoholic beverages as totally and utterly deleterious: even the occasional whisky is recommended by medical practitioners concerned about the state of a patient's heart, or possibly his blood. It's hard to keep up. It is even suggested in some quarters that the abominable cigarette protects the system against certain diseases though it is not acceptable to say it out loud. Coming from the opposite direction we have nutritionary experts uttering dire warnings about the possible effects of previously highly regarded 'natural remedies'. Overdosing on seemingly virtuous vitamins can seriously damage your health. Jogging and other forms of physical exercise are now regarded by some sages as addictive and harmful, particularly if you perform them so strenuously that you shake your internal organs loose, though I would have thought that the merest amateur of health might have already suspectd that there was something inadvisable in over-exerting the body to such an extent. The exhortation we were once daily subject to to go out into the fresh air has faded into silence as the said air is now held to be too polluted to go out into without a protective mask, and all in all listening to the advice we are offered can lead to great stress. How reassuring, therefore, to know that it is good for us. I am particularly pleased, being an Olympic-class worrier. The ozone layer, the state of the economy, the decline of the inner cities, the evasion of truth so prevalent among our leaders all serve to worry me in the small hours when I can't think of anything else to worry about, which is not often. There is always something closer to home to agitate the housewife: the curious knocking noise in the boiler, the cat's habit of throwing up on manuscripts, the best time to prune the ivy which is climbing in through the windows, in order not to discommode the doubtless protected species of wildlife which is living in it. Anything can lead to stress in those of us who are of a less than sunny and optimistic disposition. I am writing this in a pub over a half of lager and have just noticed that the manager has put some logs on top of a coal fire. I once read that a mixture of wood and coal inevitably leads to a conflagration in the chimney and am wondering when it is likely to occur. We are about to take to the motorway and as I'm not driving and so do not have that particular stress available to me I shall worry about the pub chimney all the way home.

Another Scone?

While tidying up in preparation for a family party I found some old snapshots and was struck by the style of the clothes: ladies looked matchlessly smart in tailored and hand-finished garments, silk stockings, gloves and what were frequently described in the literature of the age as 'ridiculous little hats', which were kept on the head while their owners were at lunch or tea, but not, I imagine, breakfast or dinner. I can remember the musty, powdery smell of veiling, the slither of silk and the harshness of tweed on the face should you chance to fall asleep on the knee of a gentleman. These were not much in evidence in the child's daily life, going off in the morning to their places of business and returning in the evening with their newspapers – a lowering sign that fun was over for the day and bedtime was nigh, together with a mug of disgusting hot milk. People then had firm ideas about the proper quantities of sweets the child could ingest, they made you drink your milk and take malt and cod-liver oil and eat up everything on your plate, including the fat on the mutton chop and the skin on the sago pudding. This did little lasting harm, contributing to the pleasure of growing up when you could decide for yourself whether or not you were going to eat spinach. When you are three or four it is impossible to imagine this happy state of affairs.

As a child I was not, however, unduly oppressed, spending the days when the weather was fine in rather chic cotton pyjamas and a panama hat, and playing with the cat next door whose name I hesitate to repeat. All black cats were called that in those days but it sounds most strange now. I got dragged out to tea more often than I found convenient although I don't think I was made to wear anything too special. Some unfortunate children were forced into fairy frocks and glacé kid pumps or velvet suits and shirts with frilly collars and were objects of mirth or pity, depending on the disposition of the observer. My mother regarded the over-dressed of any age with contempt, a powerful prejudice which I picked up early – detesting on sight little girls with big satin bows on their curls and very white socks and little boys with tidy hair who kept close to their mummies. I am told that my worst fault at tea parties was a tendency to scoff whole platefuls of bread and butter. This was probably because they'd cut the crusts off: at home you had to eat the crusts on the grounds that they'd make your hair curl – and it was useless to protest that you hated curly hair. It seems to me preferable to gobbling the entire Victoria sponge or all the éclairs but apparently the feelings of some hostesses were hurt when the *pièce de résistance* was not sufficiently appreciated.

I believe tea parties still go on in some parts of the country and I wish I could go to one, rather as I'd like to watch a rain dance or a neo-paleolithic fertility rite. They were probably among the most formal occasions I have ever or will ever attend. Everything changed during the war and got more casual. The stuffiest dinner party now is not more governed by ritual than the nerve-wracking thirties tea party: where the guests had to balance cup, saucer, teaspoon, napkin and plate, not splutter crumbs or squirt cream or drop the lot on the rug *and* make informed conversation about the state of the antirrhinums or the lady down the road. All the while being careful to say nothing unsuitable for the ears of the child or to make sure it was above her head. Never mind, apart from some boredom and the hot milk, being three wasn't too bad.

Meanwhile, in Another Church . . .

I did not have a very peaceful Christmas Eve. To begin with I had to make a decision about where to go for Midnight Mass. The church I used to go to now gives the impression of being run by amateurs, with occasional priests making a sort of guest appearance: people go 'hallelujah' at unexpected moments and I find it difficult to follow the course of events. I'm told it's something to do with 'empowering the laity'. Unfortunately the overall effect is faintly comic and reminiscent of a Roman saturnalia or one of those medieval festivals when the Lord of Misrule held sway. I dare say it will all calm down again in time but the goings-on are not at present an edifying spectacle.

After much thought the daughter and I decided on St James, Spanish Place: here we could lurk by the door when Mass was over and leap out at our friend Ruth (a regular attendant), thus giving her a nice surprise – or so we reasoned. We rang up a mini-cab firm and told it we required a vehicle at 11.30: it appeared at 8.30, waking me up from an exhausted slumber, for I had been messing about with parsnips and things all day, and had to be sent away again. Finally, when it arrived at the appointed time we climbed in and announced to the driver, 'Spanish Place'. 'That's in Jamaica,' he said, astounded. 'No, no,' we said, 'that's Spanish *Town*. We want

Spanish *Place* – off Marylebone High Street.' Having sorted this out we set off in the wrong direction. 'Hang on,' we cried, 'let us consult the *A to Z* and plan our route in a sensible fashion.' He was perfectly amenable and drove around for a while as the daughter and I squinted at the small print. When we were on the right road we fell into conversation: learning that we were going to Midnight Mass he decided that we would need to be brought home again and he was the man for the job. 'You'll be about an hour,' he declaimed, 'with all that sacerdotal stuff.' Here I enquired about his own interior life and religious persuasion and was informed that he had once been a Catholic but had converted to animism. Then we had a remarkably confusing discussion involving Poseidon and the Christian symbol of the fish. He'd read something about it only that day. Neither the daughter nor I were up to all this intellectual challenge and were glad when we eventually discovered our goal. It had taken some time.

When Mass was over we searched in vain for Ruth. I wanted to stay on and eat mince pies in the Social Centre but something told me not to delay the driver. I was right. The wretched man had waited for us while the fare rose steadily. He managed to give the impression that this had been thoughtful of him and you can't roar at people when you've just been to Mass: so we talked about his Christmas dinner. How – he wanted to know – should he cook his duck? He'd had a pheasant last year but his flat-mates had been cross with him because he'd left it in the fridge for ten days and it had taken on a new and distressing form of life. I told him all I knew about duck cookery, he opined that I was an opera singer by profession, I paid him and we parted amicably.

Ruth had gone to the Carmelite Church: she says it's all very well having good ideas but when the next festival comes round we might do some planning beforehand.

In the Footsteps of Marilyn Monroe

Having watched a black-and-white film made in the thirties and starring the elegant and amusing Cicely Courtneidge, I developed a theory. It goes as follows. After the Second World War something strange happened to women. During the thirties they had been progressing nicely: the more noticeable – the role models – the entertainers, actresses, writers, aristocrats, gave an impression of confidence, independence, elegance and wit. If they had their neuroses and quirks they didn't bore everyone to death by constantly airing them. The Victorian Miss and the flapper of the twenties had been left behind and a pleasantly adult female had taken their place. Sometimes she was unhappy, sometimes she committed suicide, but she didn't whine too much about the injustices done to her sex. There were social injustices to worry about, and while I must admit that some of the ladies I have in mind would not have lost much sleep over the plight of the workers, it was the wider issues that were the focus of whatever public concern there was. The small girl could hope to grow up and emulate Bette Davis, Beatrice Lillie, Katherine Hepburn or even Joan Crawford, although she was a bit *too* tough for some tastes, quelling strong men with a glance that could freeze a Martini at several paces. Women then also felt free to be funny without sacrificing glamour. Many females of powerful personality were also undeniably feminine and they cropped up everywhere.

So there we had these estimable grown-ups acting and writing and teaching and running tea shops or in domestic service or merely doing the Season, when along came the war. They were all diverted from their various occupations and went into the army, navy, nursing, munitions factories, the NAAFI or ENSA or onto the land. Husbands and sweethearts went off to fight the foe and life was never the same again. I don't know how it happened but those confident, capable ladies went out of style and never came back. Elegance in dress disappeared, Dior swept everywhere with his 'New Look' and fashion became a matter only of hemline – up or down – an obviously obsessively sexual preoccupation. The Americans invented the 'Baby Doll' female with the matching nightie and pants, and then Marilyn Monroe ended all chance of a return to sense by contriving to become everyone's dream girl. It was said that she was adored by both men and women, but I except myself. No matter what the poor woman was really like she gave the effect of being not very bright and a bit of a pushover. I strongly suspect her of being responsible for the feminist movement, for few women would wish to resemble Marilyn Monroe unless they were mad. Overweight, foolish, vulgar and designed and controlled by men is not an appealing image. I expect that what happened is that women, aghast at the thought that men would like them to teeter around in high heels and frocks that drifted up to show their knickers, rebelled in reaction, not against the history of women's subjection and ill-treatment, but against the awful prospect of being required to follow in the footsteps of Marilyn Monroe.

Not Shaken, and Not Stirred

And then there was James Bond. While Marilyn is not the ideal role model for girls, James is not the perfect exemplar for boys. For a start when he appeared on the scene he heralded the death of romance. All those women, whether they were on his side or not, kept flinging themselves at his feet and he didn't have to take any trouble at all wooing any of them. There is no tension in a story which has no element of pursuit. James and his adversaries chased each other, certainly, through all manner of hazards and complexities but the females were there on a plate, batting their eyelashes and flashing come-hither glances with the maddening regularity of fruit machines. Where was the haughty Beauty of Romance, where the dashing Cavalier? He'd dashed off somewhere else, that's where, and James had taken his place. I hate James Bond. He was no gentleman and he leapt to vulgar and unwarranted conclusions. I seem to remember him sizing up a person as not one of us because he ordered red wine with his fish. Not sufficient grounds, it seems to me, for sealing his death warrant. His dinner companion may have been public enemy number one, and in this case indeed he was, but he could have been a person who had been to too many publisher's parties and had vowed never ever under any circumstances whatsoever to ingest one more glass of white wine. And James was positively old-maidish the way he fussed over the preparation of his Martini. Well-bred people drink what they're given, how it comes, and anyway I can't see that shaking or stirring would make all that much difference to the final result. I bet James wouldn't have been able to tell if his Martini had gone round in the concrete mixer. What's more, even with his grasp of technology, I am convinced he wouldn't have been competent to change a washer on a tap. He is not the sort of person you'd want around the house on a regular basis. He'd seduce any female visitors from your aunt to the Jehovah's Witnesses and vaporize with one twist of his wrist-watch any unsuspecting guest who requested a claret with his cod. Imagine travelling with him: you'd be sitting in the car when he grew suspicious of the blue Escort in the next lane and you'd find yourself ejected onto the motorway and expected to find your own way home. In a train you'd be lost for explanation as your fellow travellers witnessed James chasing a person with iron teeth up onto the roof. Getting anywhere by BR is bad enough already without having to cope with James's neuroses. He would be a constant source of embarrassment. I'm sure that Errol Flynn and Douglas Fairbanks would have been of little practical assistance in the house, and it cannot be denied that they had a tendency to fling maidens across the pommels of their saddles and canter away with them, but their motives were pure. They wouldn't show you up by sneering at the vinous peculiarities of your guests or casually assassinating them. I think we should encourage the young to emulate the saints rather than those ill-conducted and unpredictable people.

Women Rule OK

Can I Hold My Beauty? is the title of a book we picked up in an Oxfam shop. It could be the title of an equine saga or even a 'bodice-ripper' but it is really about maintaining your personal daintiness and attractiveness with a view to keeping your man and not frightening him to death. 'Please, never take out your plate at night . . . the most important reason for not removing your teeth except to wash them is the fact that your husband would not find you beautiful without them, to say the least.' It adds that smokers must clean their teeth all the time because 'A woman whose breath reeks of nicotine immediately spoils her feminine charm.' Even if you've got your own teeth, '. . . if your mouth has become set in lines of tenseness, frigidity or bitterness, it will be necessary for you to cultivate a more generous, affectionate, responsive feeling about your life in general, before your mouth can be truly lovely. It is the inner warmth – the smile from the heart – which makes even a plain woman beautiful when she looks at or speaks of one she loves.' Oh yeah.

This book was written in 1946 and fashions change, but telling women what to do is an ingrained habit in the human race. Sometimes people tell men what to do: Arthur Mee and Lord Baden-Powell were given to advising lads about this and that, but they were mostly concerned with a different sort

19

of purity from keeping your gums in shape and avoiding halitosis. No one has taken their place unless we count those who would bring on New Man, encouraging him to cuddle trees and scream. No, it is still women who are told how to behave and it is usually other women who tell them, despite the squawks about Patriarchy and Dominançe. Now you cannot open a women's magazine without encountering suggestions – nay, directions – on how to improve your sex life, and they are very different from the strictures laid down by Veronica Dengel, the author of *Can I Hold My Beauty?* I read a tip from a woman the other day about having a 'quickie' on the ironing board. It sounded impractical: ironing boards have a tendency to fold and collapse even when you're merely ironing on them. Veronica would have found this hint bizarre and, to be honest, I do too.

Veronica is concerned with more important matters. 'I hope you are not forming the opinion that I want you to subordinate your personality to your husband's,' she says. 'Quite the contrary. It is imperative for you to maintain your individuality, develop your abilities, and become a well-rounded, nicely balanced, mature woman.' Unless, of course, you've died in your sleep from swallowing your teeth.

You mustn't use bad language either. 'A man feels that he can swear if he wants to, but he doesn't want to hear even "damn" or "hell" from his wife. Do avoid using "My God" every few sentences . . .' And you mustn't get drunk. It's not dainty. And 'Don't feel that the necessity of pawning your jewellery is a disgrace. Give it up cheerfully . . . Be gay, attractive and keep smiling.' This would be difficult in one situation Veronica describes. A man asked his bride to run his bath and she said he could run his own. He said his mother had always run it and until his wife did he wasn't going to wash. Veronica says a sense of humour helps. She

20

concludes, 'Psychologists have been able to trace unexplainable moods in a man to the fact that his wife was behaving in a way which was foreign to that of his mother.' My own conclusion is that Women Rule OK, and they always have done. Otherwise they wouldn't feel the need of constant warnings on how to behave. It is the sense of hidden female power, not weakness, that so exercises society.

The Two Beryls

We have had a hectic and faintly confusing few days. This is
partly because we have two Beryls on the premises: one a dog
and one a distinguished novelist. I shriek, 'Beryl, stop that at
once,' and the novelist jumps a foot in the air; I say, 'Beryl,
would you like a drink?' and the dog looks interested. The
hectic aspect arises out of the fact that Beryl the dog has four
puppies, Brutus, Tertius, Alfie and Martha, imps of Satan all
of them. They chew hand luggage, toes, each other's legs,
ears and tails, and have not yet grasped any of the finer points
of the concepts of obedience, good manners or basic hygiene.
You come down in the morning and find yourself stumbling
through a shifting tide of puppies nipping at your nightdress
and demanding food and games: their teeth would once have
been compared to gramophone needles but there is nothing
so sharply pointed in the technology of today. There is
nothing as sharp as puppies' teeth in all my experience. They
are also a splendid source of worry. When you can't see one
you wonder whether it's eating someone's cashmere cardigan
or getting lost on the mountainside or in the nettles. Even
their mother is getting fed up with them and chastises them
quite roughly when she considers their behaviour has become
insupportable. Still, when they're asleep they are perfectly
adorable: little Jack Russells, mostly white but with patches

of black and brown more or less arbitrarily distributed. The prettiest have brown and black faces which give their eyes a large and lustrous appearance, while the plainest has a white domed forehead and appears a bit of a thug – small-eyed and mean-looking, which is unfair since he has a charming nature. This is why so many human beings wear eye make-up. It softens the overall rather threatening effect given by beady eyes staring out of a naked countenance. Finding myself in reflective vein I wonder what else, apart from the value of a certain amount of maquillage, we could learn from these freshly painted creatures. They relax very competently, their paws go entirely limp and floppy when they're asleep and although they occasionally utter a small yelp you know they're not troubled somewhere in their unconscious about the consequences of imposing VAT on fuel, or the fate of the rain forests. Most people are always agitating themselves about something or other even when they're supposed to be resting. On the negative side the puppies tend to be unnecessarily quarrelsome, growling and snarling in an infantile fashion and annoying each other more than seems reasonable. If they were human you'd feel that without proper guidance they might grow up to be members of the BNP. However, they are all going to good homes where, I trust, their anti-social attitudes will be curbed. Their enthusiasm is admirable and, properly channelled, will doubtless prove of benefit to society. And when they stream out after the master of the house as he takes them for a walk they are as pretty as a picture. I still prefer cats but little dogs have an undeniable charm.

Enough of canines. I must turn my attention to the novelist and give her a drink. Some human beings are delightful too, although I'd never keep one as a pet.

An Immorality Tale

Yet again there is a spirit of madness abroad in the air: an overall neuroris, sometimes approaching psychosis, which pops up in all manner of unexpected ways and places, startling the average citizen out of his habitual torpor and sometimes causing him to exclaim aloud or write letters to the paper. I am constantly surprised at the patience of the population harassed by ever-proliferating bureaucracy, flung out of work to the accompaniment of self-righteous lectures on the sacred nature of profit and the interests of share-holders, and required to be loyal to a caste of people who are selfish, greedy, dishonest, remote from ordinary life and incapable of telling the truth. The most worrying aspect is that to so many in positions of authority common sense is a totally foreign quality. It wouldn't matter much that most of our leaders are pretty poor specimens of humanity if only they showed some sign of being acquainted with reality. If we'd been asked we could have told them that comprehensive schooling was a bad idea, that high-rise ghettos were a bad idea, that the slackening of discipline in hospitals was a bad idea, that the Channel Tunnel is a bad idea and, all things considered, that the EEC is a lousy idea. I weep with sympathy when I read of farmers who have no time to milk the cow or feed the chickens because they've got too many forms to fill in and have to measure the paddock, and I get cross when I read of others who are living the life of Riley because they've filled in their forms in a highly imaginative fashion. The urge to centralization is lovely for bureaucrats and deadly for people, and social engineering, manipulation from the top, always ends in disaster and tears. So there.

But the madness seeps in in other ways. The insistence that we are all much the same, regardless of sex, is a rich source of barminess. There was a recent TV programme in which a woman who had been raped spoke to a man who had raped. It was suggested that since he, at the age of twelve, had been interfered with by a girl of sixteen, then their experiences had been similar. It is possible, although perhaps a little improbable, that he had thoroughly disliked the occurrence, but it is not the same as brutal rape. At the other extreme, just the other day a person reviewed a book about paedophilia in sympathetic terms, claiming that the author's heart was in the right place because he differentiated between gentle men who really loved children and nasty men who only exploited them. No pre-pubertal child, subjected to sexual abuse by an adult, no matter how shy and gentle, is going to get anything but disgust, fear and guilt from it and anyone who claims differently is suffering from acute withdrawal from reality. The move to de-mystify sex and make it available to all as no more than a form of pleasant recreation is greatly lacking in common sense. So is the idea recently put forward by a teacher that his pupils would benefit more from reading Edwin Morgan's poem about gang rape than about Wordsworth's daffodils. I was never mad about daffodils but they have the edge over gang rape when it comes to the English lesson.

High Spirits

I'm sitting on an aeroplane, wondering why. I hate aeroplanes. On the other hand they do get you from place to place nice and quickly. I went to Poland on a train once, which was a big mistake, and I've been on buses to various places – a mode of travel that in my opinion leaves a lot to be desired. They always go too fast down motorways and round corners and yet take too long to get you to your destination. You can grow desperately bored on a bus unless it's overtaking something in the fast lane. Statistically speaking – or so we are told by those who wish us, for whatever motive, to fly around in the air – planes offer by far the safest means of getting from hither to yon. I'll pause here for a moment while I explain this to the person next to me since we're about to take off and she's wondering, even more fervently than I am myself, why she's here. Because it only takes four hours to get us home is the answer. Imagine how long it must have taken the Crusaders to get from Heathrow to the Holy Land and back. However, they would not have been subjected to interrogation at the point of departure, which must have saved them some time, and they probably had someone to carry the luggage.

There is something about my appearance and demeanour which arouses suspicion in the breasts of security personnel. I phoned home to say I'd arrived safely in Tel Aviv and it was pretty surprising because for a while it looked as though I wouldn't be permitted out of the airport in England, and my son said that there was nothing new about that: I was always the one to be stopped and searched and closely questioned. The portals through which one is required to pass to prove oneself bomb- and weapon-free scream at my earrings, and customs officials all over the world have patted me in the expectation of finding hidden contraband.

This time getting through security took three quarters of an hour. First I was interrogated by a young man, who, for some reason I could not fathom, then went away with my passport and was replaced by two young women, who asked me the same questions and then some more. 'Why,' they enquired, 'was I going to Israel?' I let myself down here because there were several reasons and I proceeded to give them all. The rule should be to offer *one* answer, precisely as in making excuses for not going to a party: more than one gives rise to doubt of your veracity, since even if it's true no one would believe that you had broken your ankle *and* been unexpectedly visited by old acquaintances from out of town.

Then they asked where exactly I was going and I let myself down again because I said I was going to lots of places only I couldn't remember where, and my chum, who by now had been cleared and was sitting, waiting, tapping her foot, was in charge of the itinerary. 'Are you looking forward to your trip?' asked the girls cunningly. 'Oh enormously,' I said. Their eyes gleamed with triumph and they leaned towards me, balancing on their knuckles on the interrogation table. 'Why,' they demanded, 'when you don't know where you're going?' I responded stiffly that I had been led to believe that most of the place was highly delightful and I anticipated nothing but interest, stimulation and pleasure. They let me through eventually, but it was a close-run thing.

I have just committed the error of looking out of the window, thus reminding myself of our unnatural situation: the secret of air travel is to forget you're doing it and pretend you're on a bus. Even if it's statistically more hazardous, ground travel seems more plausible. Here comes lunch. The other secret of air travel is never to eat the food because it always makes you feel ill.

The Holy Land

We had an interesting time in the Holy Land. When we arrived it was raining cats and dogs so I had to buy new boots since espadrilles were not suited to the present state of the climate: the heels wore down as we plodded round the Old City of Jerusalem in the wake of Shimshon (Sampson), our guide for the day. He had to keep waving a red scarf above the heads of the crowd to indicate his whereabouts, explaining nonchalantly that he had, in the past, lost a few tourists. In the Church of the Holy Sepulchre we were seized by a freelance guide wearing a furry hat with ear flaps. 'What religion are you?' he demanded. 'RC,' said I. 'Jewish,' said my friend. 'Me too,' said ear flaps. We considered going back and telling him we were followers of Baal and waiting to hear how he'd respond. However, he was as nothing compared to the next guide we encountered. This was a young American with whiskers whom we met in a hotel. 'I,' he announced, 'will take you to the parts other guides cannot reach.' Innocently we thought this would be rather nice, so together with another lady from the hotel, we followed him out of the Jaffa Gate and down a hill. At one point his anorak fell aside to reveal that he was carrying a gun. We should have been warned but it seemed too late to turn back so we went on. Next thing we knew we were being piled into an armoured jeep manned by two more gun-toting characters, and were driving along what might have been a road until the rains washed it away. We stopped by a school playground full of little Arab children and were ushered to a flight of steps leading down to a hole containing some water. 'That,' said the guide triumphantly, 'is Hezekiah's Tunnel, a magnificent feat of engineering.' We were less appreciative than we might have been, having realized that we were in the City of David where we had been told, by older and wiser people, not, on any account, to go anywhere near. And the jeep had driven off. As we stood there, thinking unholy thoughts about our guide, a car came lurching through the pot holes and stopped in front of us. No one got out. It just stayed there for what felt like half an hour while we gazed round at the desolation and chattered inconsequentially about the extraordinary brilliance of good old Hezekiah.

The occupants of the car must have finally decided we were just boring tourists with a passion for looking down holes in the ground and went away again: but none of us was feeling in the least bit grateful to, and far from fond of, the guide. How we missed Shimshon who would not have dreamed of endangering us, although he did take us to places like the diamond factory and the kitsch shops in the hope, since he would get a cut, that we'd all go mad and purchase mounds of jewellery and plastic representations of the Baby Jesus in a gold embroidered nappy, a nylon bob and a halo.

On the way home our City of David guide kept us waiting for hours in a leather shop while he chose a new holster. We all decided that he had a wistful yearning to get involved in a shoot-out and we didn't even buy him a drink. Just goes to show how careful you must be about false prophets and guides.

Cat-owner's Blues

Drat the cat. And while I'm at it, drat a few other people's cats as well. The tiresomeness of felines fills me with fellow-feeling (I didn't mean to write a sentence with all those effs: I must be tired). Cat-owners can have a hard time. The politically correct, who are now well over the brink of madness and almost out of sight, tell us that we must not think of ourselves as 'owners' or even speak of 'pets': we must refer to our 'animal companions'. All very fine and large but Puss at present is nobody's companion. She is Home Alone. We were staying in the country and when the time came to leave she did a runner – as the young so graphically describe it. This is because she loathes travelling, but then don't we all. I especially dislike travelling with Puss since she behaves in a fashion which necessitates opening all the car windows. We put up with it in a spirit of Christian forbearance but she is a disobedient and ungrateful beast and has caused great trouble and inconvenience by refusing to return with us. Daily the vicar's wife and the plumber have to go round with meals on wheels, and in order to show her that we *care* I have instructed them to spend some time sitting down and socializing with her. Before she ambled insouciantly home and miaowed at the plumber, who was up there plying his trade, I lay awake for hours picturing terrible scenes of tragedy involving weasels, foxes, owls, farm dogs and gamekeepers. I was quite worn out. To add to the annoyance I could not forget that I'd just paid the vet a huge sum of money, plus VAT, to have her health checked. She is an old cat (although you wouldn't know it from the way she carries on) and great clumps of fur were falling off her and collecting in corners. She was definitely follically challenged. Also her teeth were clicking as she ate. The vet anaesthetized her, worked on the teeth, injected her with various substances and then X-rayed her. This process revealed that she had only one kidney and no one has any idea what happened to the other one.

I have a friend who also possesses – no, sorry – shares her life and home with an old lady cat who is similarly reckless. This animal, one Tina, looks incapable of wild adventure, being fat – sorry – nutritionally challenged, yet periodically goes off on nocturnal trips looking for something to fight. She returns in deplorable condition and the vet makes yet more vast sums. I was astonished, looking at Tina, to hear of her proclivities. As I remarked at the time, you'd as soon expect the Queen Mother to go out looking for trouble. Tina very much resembles the Queen Mother in demeanour until the moon is high, when her baser instincts assert themselves. Puss, on the other hand, resembles more one of the cast of *EastEnders*: one of those plucky old girls (I have given up trying to be politically correct) whom you wouldn't cross in a hurry.

I know of two other cats who, although adored by their owner, cause her endless grief. They catch rats and bring them home alive or dead and she's not sure which is worse, chasing live rats or sweeping up their dismembered components. Erik, if he has caught a mouse, tends to unravel it up the hallway, and if he has caught a rat, eats most of it but leaves a tail, a foot and a head in artistically arranged order for the householder to dispose of. This sheds an interesting light on feline attitudes. Erik and his friend Cesare, whose party piece is sitting on his owner's neck while she types (he will probably be reading this) are both male, yet more concerned with bringing in things to eat, doing the shopping as it were, while the female cats seem hell-bent on endangering themselves by sallying forth on deeds of valour or merely behaving recklessly. I don't know what a feminist reading of this would be but it baffles me.

When You Knew Who Was Right

A member of the household has just announced, rather brokenly, that all she wants is an abacus. Her computer has been giving her lip. She told it to do something and it said it wouldn't. She re-phrased her request and it said she was doing it wrong and suggested she do something else. So she did and it indicated with smug triumph that it wasn't going to respond to that either. So there. I knew a horse like that once.

Reflecting on these matters we arrive by a roundabout route at the question of authority. What is it and where does it reside? I used to know: in the maths mistress was where, and the geography mistress and She Who Taught Us Latin. The word of these ladies was law and you'd no sooner disobey a command than fly in the air. You invariably addressed them in formal terms and if they had Christian names we didn't know what they were.

It was different when our children came of an age to attend places of learning. The teachers were known by their first names and any authority they might once have possessed had been put aside in the interests of democracy or something. We never did quite figure out why it was considered so liberating to let the pupils rampage about using naughty language and refusing to do their sums.

A surprising number of them are dead now and some are in

prison – at least one for murder. Only one of my contemporaries has done time (as far as I know) and he's an accountant: well brought up but a touch too cute with the sums. He went to a boys' school and so lacked the influence of our maths mistress, who would have ensured that not only did he get the figures correct but put them in the right columns.

We were polite to policemen too, treating them – now I look back – with a mixture of respect and hauteur. They were both guardians of the law and servants of the public. We were on the right side of the former and constituted the latter, so everyone knew where they were.

And we were breathtakingly polite to nuns, standing aside to let them pass on the street and ushering them first on the buses. No one said a rude word in their presence. You could tell they were nuns by the way they were dressed. Now it is sometimes difficult to distinguish a nun from a *fille de joie* or a truck-driver and they don't seem to carry the same authority. Especially not when they're doing circle-dancing.

And as for priests: well, we tended to do what they told us, confident that, in most cases, they were in their right minds and backed by the authority of the Church. I cannot imagine speaking to one as I now sometimes have occasion to: 'But look here, pet, we gave up worshipping the earth-goddess some time go. Aren't you being a bit old-hat?'

It is difficult to pay respect to a person in a T-shirt telling you earnestly that the Red Indians had got it right and the Fathers of the Church all wrong while implying that you must be half-witted not to take his word for it. The more way-out clerics remind one of the rogue computer. Their programming is all awry and you can't get a proper response to a proper question.

And if we're going to haul the horse into this metaphor, all I can say is I wouldn't put money on one of them.

Pillar to Post

Every so often the post gets annoying. As you pick it up first
thing on Monday morning you know at a glance it will not
contain cheques or letters from loved ones or from long-lost
friends or any good news at all: it will consist of bills and
circulars and begging letters and communications from mad
people who wish to let you know that they are being rayed by
members of the government and royal family and ask what
you're going to do about it. Possibly the most infuriating are
those bills which come complete with messages of self-praise
from the organization concerned. 'We did extensive research
into how we could improve the design of the phone bill. And,
naturally, we asked you, our customers, what you thought
and what you wanted on the new bill.' No one asked me or
I'd have told them. 'Lower charges', is what I would have
said, and they could forget the *Network Services* – such as Call
Waiting, Call Barring and Three-way Calling'. I don't know
what they mean by these terms but they all sound like a neat
way to make life more confusing and expensive. If I wish to
make a call I pick up the phone and dial the number, if I
don't wish to receive calls I take the phone off the hook.
Simple.

Water boards also make a fearful song and dance about
what they're up to, sending you boring pamphlets on the

subject. Water is a basic essential of life but I can think of more interesting things to read about: '. . . taps you use for garden hoses must have a double check valve fitted to stop drinking water being contaminated and from January 1993 all new toilets must not use more than 7.5 litres to flush.' As you waft away the smell of chlorine from your early morning cup of tea you wish they'd just shut up and get on with it, especially if they're outside digging holes in the road while they tinker with the sewage system. You open a large envelope and out falls a glossy brochure on the subject of breast cancer. You've just heard an expert telling you that, on the whole, breast screening has proved sadly ineffective in preventing the spread of the disease so you don't know who to believe, although the costly nature of the document before you makes you faintly suspicious of its motives. *Qui bono?* Open another envelope and you have another glossy brochure – about a motor car this time. They want you to test-drive it. As I've never driven this could prove interesting. They go on to tell you that their product offers you the best of both worlds and you wonder which worlds they have in mind. In my case it would be out of this one and swiftly into the next. So to the bin with all this garbage and you turn to the letters with the unfamiliar hand-writing and the foreign postmarks. A German gentleman wants your autograph. He writes with courtly foreign grace, '*Sehr geehrte gnädige Frau . . .* ' and goes on to request your *Handschriftensammlung*. Your once-innocent nature having by now been corrupted by doubt, you wonder if he's worked out some smart way of affixing your signature to a cheque and he too goes into the bin. Then comes the one to finally put you off your cornflakes. An ex-private detective in an ex-communist country has been cheated into bank-ruptcy by some evil men and is desperate for money. Unfortunately he appears to need US$280,000 which is beyond most people's means. He describes his plans to travel abroad and wreak vengeance on his enemies. The country he cites is notorious for bad faith in business deals and his letter has the awful ring of truth. He concludes, 'You are our last bright heavenly gleam in the immense deadly black world.' He threatens to shoot himself and his letter is going to haunt me. I don't want to ruin anyone's morning by begging but is there a millionaire out there who could help?

Apologia

I am not a good correspondent. I have detested letter-writing since the days when I was compelled to sit down immediately after Christmas or a birthday and think of some new way of saying 'thank you' for some anthology of kiddies' verse or box of hankies. Quite often I was pointedly given coloured stationery with buttercups and bunnies simpering in the corners of the pages. Yuk. I was made to answer letters too and I always put it off for as long as I could. However, this topic is on my mind because some of you must think me the rudest person in epistolary history. Through a bizarre mischance, I have received no letters from readers. I know they have been sent but I don't know where they went. Another of life's mysteries, like the way the towels and the teaspoons disappear. Sheets and dinner knives also have a curious habit of dematerializing and no solution ever presents itself. And as for socks – but there, everyone loses socks in an inexplicable manner and I could go on about it for hours.

Please consider this an apology for my failure to respond, though it is really more a reason because, for once, it isn't my fault. Some of the letters that do get through to me from other sources are very strange, defying rational response. People want me to send them money to help finance new religions that they have just thought up, or to enable them to pursue villains who have wronged them. The bankrupt Bulgarian private detective is the most intriguing to date, but the oddest of all is yet another German gentleman who has sent letters to every writer he has ever heard of, offering to leave them his fortune in return for their signatures. We have puzzled long and hard over this one: it seems an unnecessarily elaborate means of filling an autograph book. Are our signatures of any monetary value, and if so why aren't we all collecting each other's? We wondered whether, within the European Community, there was now a means of affixing other people's signatures to various sorts of money order, since forgery is apparently quite simple with the rise of new technologies. Sadly there is no way of ascertaining this without sending him a signature and waiting to see what happens to one's bank account. Then it occurred to us that A.T.E. doesn't have a bank account so we sent him a scrawl in the hope that he'll let us know what he's doing with it. We wanted to beg him to let us in on the scam but we didn't think he would. People when asked, 'Come on – tell us what the game is', seldom offer a straightforward answer. It is yet another of life's little mysteries.

Another thing that surprises me is that some people appear to like writing letters: they like having a number of pen pals and sending off screeds on a regular basis. One of my correspondents lives in the heart of Africa and is a young seminarian. I answer his letters because I have an idea that when he grows up he might make a good Pope and I want to ensure that he doesn't fall for any of the daffier modernist notions that are floating around in the Western World. It seems to me desirable that the Pope should be a Catholic and to this end I am prepared to fill envelopes and lick stamps.

All my letters begin, 'I'm sorry not to have written earlier', and they end, unless they're going to the bank manager, 'Lots of love from Alice'. Please take this personally unless, of course, you've written to me in green ink hoping I'll be excommunicated.

A Stranger in the Border

A purple flower has sprung up in the garden. I'm quite sure I didn't put it there and I don't know what its name is. For some obscure and doubtless potty reason this causes me to rather resent it. I felt the same way about a tree that secretly seeded itself and grew twenty feet tall before suddenly producing a bunch of keys and shaking them insistently in the breeze, thus proclaiming itself an ash. Now I know what it is I regard it as one of the family rather than an interloper. I don't mind weeds, indeed I rather admire their cheek, as long as I know what they're called. Dandelions and daisies and even chickweed look quite pretty, and a simply enormous bank of nettles and thistles can be almost a source of pride. You tell people they're part of your set-aside scheme, put there to encourage butterflies and other species of wildlife, but let some alien and nameless plant seize upon your territory and the tendency is to put paraquat on it: not that I would ever do such a thing for I have heard too many horror stories about paraquat. It is vitally important to keep it in a container clearly labelled with its *name* and not in an old ginger beer bottle where it can masquerade as an innocent substance. I wouldn't be at all surprised if the politically correct regarded this as fascist and unfair to weedkiller, loath as they are to call a spade a spade.

The naming of names began in a garden and is clearly of great psychological significance to mankind. Most people think long and hard before they name their children and in some cases it would be better if they didn't, or at least checked on the significance of the chosen nomenclature before committing themselves (and the unfortunate kiddy) irrevocably. For instance I know of one couple who called their daughter Simony because they thought Simone frenchified and affected. It sounds pretty but then so do Chlamydia and Syphilis. I know another couple who named a child Sunshine, which was great as long as she was beaming from her pram but will not seem so appropriate should she grow into a bad-tempered party activist of whatever persuasion. I was once asked to sign a book and, on asking the lady what her name was, found myself baffled. 'How do you spell it?' I enquired. 'T-R-E-E,' she responded, looking at me as though I had learning difficulties. I suppose it's no odder than Sky but it's unexpected when you're used to people having people's names. There was an old Liverpool story about a girl called Hazel – 'All the Saints in the calender and they had to go and call her after a nut.' We had problems when our children were born, sticking to family names and Saints' days wherever possible until the seventh came along, by which time I'd decided to number them. He was going to be called Septimus Henry until he turned out to be a girl, whereupon we took the line of least resistance and called her after the doctor who'd delivered her. Luckily the obstetrician was female, so that was all right.

Now I have a game for you. What do the PC call a spade? So far we've come up with 'a person-made implement to be used in a caring fashion on mother-earth after first having communed with her and requested her permission to . . .' Here I tried to think of a euphemism for 'dig a hole' and gave up.

As to the flower in the garden – if I can't find its description in a book I'm going to call it Felix. The cat's called Basil so it seems only fair.

Red Rag to a Psychotherapist

I dreamed that BR kept a black bull as a pet on Euston Station: it was perfectly harmless, the officials assured us, as long as it wasn't irritated by small dogs. Why my unconscious had to attribute this added, unlikely inconvenience to the annoyances of travel by rail is something I am not qualified to discover. It would have made more sense if I had dreamed of small dogs but, despite the insistence of the followers of Freud, the unconscious seldom does make sense. Nor do certain publicans. The previous evening we had stopped at a pleasant-looking inn, with an early Georgian appearance and honeysuckle around the door, and gone eagerly inside hoping to be served swiftly with a soothing glass of beer. With us was Bertie, who is the small dog of one of our company. The interior of the pub in no way lived up to the promise of its exterior; it had the worst, most unwelcoming sort of modern furniture, an electrical log lit by a lamp bulb, and there was no one behind the bar. For a quite considerable time there was no one behind the bar so the owner of Bertie, who is not a patient person, went to look for someone. Presently a lady appeared and requested that we put Bertie on a lead since people might come in demanding food. We thought this improbable in the extreme and I couldn't see why Bertie on a lead would be more hygienic than a free-ranging Bertie but said nothing. His owner, however, remarked in a tone nicely poised between simple enquiry and guarded truculence that she thought she had noticed, when she looked in the kitchen, one of those fluffy little numbers with pop eyes. 'That's right,' said the bar tender, leaning her elbows on the bar, 'a Pekingese.' We gathered from her demeanour that it would be unwise to pursue the topic and went outside to sit in the evening chill. It's years since I saw a Pekingese. Fashions in dogs change as much as fashions in anything else. I remember a lady who was so fond of her Pekingeses that when they died she had them stuffed and continued to take them everywhere – the Ritz, the Savoy, everywhere. Before that Scotties were all the rage: ladies would keep two as pets and wear scarves and blouses printed with pictures of Scottie dogs, and brooches in the form of Scottie dogs, and hang their portraits on the walls. They were bad-tempered little creatures but few people would acknowledge this, wearing forced smiles as they shook them free of their ankles. Bertie is a Jack Russell terrier and a well-disposed animal. Beryl too is a Jack Russell terrier and she is the reason I wouldn't be surprised to find my slumbers disturbed by dreams of small dogs. She is what is known in Yiddish as a *rachmonis*. Now my spoken Yiddish is coming along by leaps and bounds but I can't spell it so I apologize if I've got it wrong. It means the sort of person who bursts into tears if people aren't talking to her, the sort who needs constant reassurance and cowers in a corner if she suspects she is being insufficiently appreciated. It puts a terrible strain on everyone else's nervous system. You have to break off in the middle of interesting conversations in order to include her and treat her with more warmth than you'd offer to your very best friend. 'How's Beryl?' is the first question you ask when you telephone. The fact that she's always just fine is somehow no comfort, for you know how impossible it is to persuade *her* of this. My nightmare is that her owners will suddenly decide to go off and explore the Amazon and leave me to look after her. The responsibility would be more than I could bear; the neurotic rage followed by suicidal depression if I was nice to the cat, the look in her eyes if I was late with her lunch, the bitter tears if I wouldn't let her sleep on my bed – and I wouldn't. There are limits after all. The worst aspect is that I sometimes have to travel by train, which is always a sore trial, and what will I do when I get to Euston Station and the black bull sees her? If I had any faith at all in the followers of Freud this is the moment when I'd go off and consult one.

The Expert's Expert

I heard a man on the wireless say, 'We have to believe the experts.' What can he mean? Nobody I know has believed an expert for longer than I care to remember. An expert only has to open his mouth for the populace to lift its lip and ask who he thinks he's kidding. Politicians, economists, architects, doctors, art critics, philosophers and certain theologians have a tendency to grow enamoured of a theory and, forsaking all others, cling to it through thick and thin. Not content with this they try to persuade the rest of us of the eternal truth of their pet notion even when water can be seen pouring out of it from every fault line. They insist on its invincible integrity and get quite cross when we laugh. The expert is almost invariably at total odds with common sense. Take the trendier educationalists who seem to think it a sadistic imposition to make children learn anything, take the planners who have destroyed our inner cities, take the philosophers who put all their faith in reason, take the politicians who have subjected us to the deep-litter mode of paper bureaucracy, take the critics who endeavour to persuade us of the profound artistic interest of a floorful of rice, take the theologians who remove the theo and leave us with a lot of logy, take any expert but don't take his word for it.

The man on the wireless was insisting that pornographic

videos do not have a tendency to deprave and corrupt because the experts said so. An ounce of common sense should tell us that letting muck into our minds is on a par with welcoming cockroaches into the kitchen. We may not be inspired to follow their example, scuttling in and out of the wainscoting, burrowing into the blancmange and exuding an unpleasant odour, but their presence is a nuisance, unhygienic, and deleterious to the quality of life. Anyway, take almost any topic and you'll find that in the course of time experts have veered from pole to pole in their opinion of it. One tiny example: the dieticians of Victoria's time demanded that cabbage be boiled for hours to neutralize its unwholesome qualities. Now they insist that we merely show it the hot water, or toss it round in a wok for the briefest possible moment or, best of all, consume it raw.

On a less insignificant level, only five minutes ago there were deafening squawks about the authoritative, repressive nature of *Veritatis Splendor*, whereas now, with horrible reminders of the possibility of original sin, there begin to be loud mutterings about the failure of the Church of England to point out the difference between right and wrong.

Then there's the rhythm method of birth control, long the object of contemptuous disbelief. Suddenly it's being suggested that it actually works, something the Jews have taken for granted with their 'two weeks on, two weeks off'. They have used it to maximize their fertility and enhance their relationships. If God in His wisdom (or nature in hers, if you prefer the pagan approach) has so ordered the female cycle, it seems perverse to reject the benefits and fill the body with chemicals instead. I'm all for chemicals but only if they're really necessary in the cause of making you well. And I'm going to have butter for lunch with a small baked potato floating in it because while one expert tells you butter is bad, another says butter substitutes are worse. I don't really believe either of them but I *hate* margarine.

PS. Now the experts *do* say that porno videos have a tendency to deprave and corrupt.

All Change

'Reformers' are commonly distinguished by arrogance, ignorance, fanaticism and naivety. They have a biased, partial and misinformed view of all that has gone before and are intent on its destruction. 'We know what's best for you,' they say, trampling all over your cherished heritage with a self-righteous fervour. The Chinese Red Guard are a good example. Fr John McGowan is another. 'We priests have had no less than two years studying liturgy,' he writes. 'The vast majority of lay people have not had this privilege. It is therefore our responsibility to teach them. If they trust us, then one day they will see and understand and be grateful.' Well Heavens to Betsy – I thought – falling limply into a chair. Two thousand years of accretion of error and, at last, Fr McGowan with his two years studying liturgy has appeared to put us right. Lucky old us. He was kindly explaining to us why the re-ordering of churches is a good thing, and why the tabernacle should be put 'somewhere else. Somewhere dignified like a side chapel' so that it won't be the 'centre of attention' during the Mass, which we must now regard, if I get his drift, as only 'a shared meal'. Apart from the sensitive shrinking occasioned by this horrid phrase, I am perturbed by the apparent dismissal of the concept of the Sacrifice. What, I want to know – indeed I *demand* to know – is going on?

Craig Brown in an aside only recently made the point that it was the doctrine of transubstantiation which had always divided the Catholic from the Protestant persuasion, assuming that this was still the case. Is it? I have spoken to several priests whose eyes roll shiftily at mention of the term. 'Well, it all depends on what you *mean* by transubstantiation,' they say, seemingly fearful of appearing old-fashioned, unecumenical or merely credulous. The vandalism consequent on much of the re-ordering is bad enough, but this is ridiculous. I am still reeling from the impact of a letter I received a few years ago from a young man who had visited a Catholic seminary in Holland. He had been told, on asking if they could not have Benediction, 'We don't worship bread here.' He had then himself been asked, 'Don't you realize the Church in Holland has been almost completely protestantized?'

To confuse matters further I have spoken to several Anglican clergymen who revere the Pope far more than many RCs do, believe implicitly in the Real Presence and say Mass in the Roman rite. One of them goes round in a biretta and is busily stuffing his church with statues and icons discarded in the re-ordering of our own unfortunate edifices. Maybe the time has come to cry 'All Change': our devout Anglican brethren should be welcomed with open arms to help restore the Faith to what it was, while our reformers should be invited to step outside and share their meals elsewhere. When I feel the impulse stealing over me to share a meal (although my aesthetic sense would never permit me to put it quite like that), I book a table in a restaurant. And when I feel the need to be in the presence of the sacred I go to church. Not, I must add, one that has been re-ordered, for soon, if the reformers have their way, we will need a map and metal detector to track down the tabernacle. There is no sense of the numinous in these stripped and denuded husks.

Matriarchs who Ruled the Roost

The time has come – say many enthusiasts – to ordain women and thus 'enrich the priesthood'. This is another of those phrases which causes delicate flinching in people of a sensitive disposition: it has strong culinary connotations ('the sauce may be enriched by the addition of a can of concentrated chicken soup') and is rather touchingly intended to disarm those who would otherwise be tempted to use, in place of the word 'enrich', the word 'change' or possibly 'ruin'.

Women – said the proponents of women priests – will bring to the overly patriarchal ministry those feminine qualities of caring, tenderness and understanding. Women – they suggested – will not be authoritarian. Some of those who spoke of specifically female qualities also hold that there is no significant difference between men and women, which is confusing, but never mind.

What really strikes the impartial observer is the conviction that those who think women incapable of authoritarianism can never have met any. Do they not have mothers or aunts? Have they never encountered schoolmistresses, nurses, doctors, shopkeepers, lawyers, tax collectors? Where in the world did they get the idea that women are not bossy? I have never met a man, no matter how patriarchal, who could outdo a determined woman in terms of sheer terror. Take Mrs

Thatcher. She could reduce strong men to tears with a glance while no one is scared of John Major, who seems a gentle, friendly little soul by comparison. My mother was the youngest of seven sisters and they were all magnificently bossy with a rooted sense of their own worth and self-rightness. I was frequently cheeky to my uncles but never to my aunts – I would have been taking my life in my hands. Nor was my mother one to put up with any nonsense. Matriarchs all, they ruled their roosts and there was no court of appeal.

Now the parishioners of Auchtermuchty are having trouble with their minister, the Rev Anne Fraser, a lady with a mind of her own, who has declined to attend the Remembrance Day services at the local war memorial, banned Brownies' banners from the church and refused to let a local choir sing there. She has also banned the Nativity play from the church, and a hundred members of her congregation have demanded that she be sacked. In a petition to St Andrews Presbytery they claim, among other things, that she has broken her induction vows to promote harmony within the congregation and will not accept that she is the cause of the dissatisfaction within the church. The point is, I gather, that the Rev Anne is a *pacifist*. This is undoubtedly very funny but is also sad, and if I lived in Auchtermuchty I would not be amused.

A dangerous aspect of human nature is its propensity to tinker, to meddle with time-hallowed structure and insist on mending that which is not broken. One of my friends, himself the grandson of a Church of Scotland (male) minister, wrote in his book *The Loss of the Good Authority* about the destructive tendency of the New Broom, the impulse of the individual to make his (or, of course, her) mark by ripping out the valued old fixtures and fittings, replacing them with the untried and frequently meretricious and raising great clouds of dust.

This gives them the feeling that they are doing something.

As indeed they are – causing misery and disruption. Priests above all should be the guardians of tradition and structure.

There are meddlers and wreckers enough in every other walk of life.

A Matter of Temperament

I do not delight in every aspect of creation: certain aspects of creation are a pain in the neck; mud, mosquitoes, politicians and the month of August for a start. And people who *do* delight in every aspect of creation to carry on with. Three o'clock in the morning is another aspect I could do without. I'm sure the Lord has His own good reasons for all these, but I don't imagine He had my comfort in mind when He thought them up. No sirree. 'Ach,' say people with whiskers and bottle-bottom glasses. 'Vot you are sufferink from is clinical depression.' 'No I'm not,' I respond. My condition is characterized by apathy, agoraphobia and an inclination to make people run out and buy me Belgian chocolates and I don't call it depression. I call it being fed up. It is deplorable but there it is. '*Accidie*' it used to be called, or possibly '*tedium vitae*' and it is, I fear, a matter of temperament. I have Finnish ancestors and read recently that many Finns living deep in the forests, far from gaining delight from their proximity to Mother Nature, are given to hanging themselves from convenient boughs. God rest their souls. I think a lot of them are Lutherans too, which can't do much to cheer them up.

But then the movement known as Creation Spirituality doesn't cheer *me* up. It fills me with gloom for much of it is codswallop and all of it based on misplaced optimism. I've

56

been reading the transcript of an interview with Matthew Fox, its prime mover, and he has much to answer for. My mood wasn't nearly so bad until I came across this interview. He denies the concept of original sin and recommends a lot of ecstasy. Yes, yes, I know creation is blessed because God made it – stands to reason – but no amount of circle-dancing, tree-kissing, drum-beating, or even drugs and drink, would improve my temporal condition or that of my immortal soul. Nor would ritually reverencing X-rays of my liver and lights – one of the practices he has thought up. There are few things that would make me more despondent than contemplating all that offal. When I pass the more explicit butchers' shops I avert the eyes.

Fox appears to hold that God is related to the world as mind is to body, but since philosophers and psychologists are endlessly scrapping over how mind *is* precisely related to body that doesn't get us very far either. He says disapprovingly, 'All theism sets up a model or paradigm of people here and God "out there",' and seems to indentify Mother Earth with Jesus Christ, which is where I give up trying to follow his thought processes. Do many of us see the Eucharist as the 'sacrament of the wounded earth'? I'm damned if I do. So many heresies have crept into our daily life and infected much of the clergy that it's hard to disentangle one from another. Sometimes I get the impression that the Tinkerbell theory is taking over: that the existence of God is dependent on our own existence and perceptions. A really super-depressing thought, devoid of hope or comfort.

Now I must try and get into a better frame of mind for Christmas. It is partly the materialistic elements of the approach to the festival – by which I mean principally the endless shopping – which has made me so ill-tempered. But even if the Bishop of Durham, David Jenkins, (who I must admit is always good for a laugh, thus doing his bit towards easing the boredom) is inclined to deny the idea of the Second Coming, at least we can celebrate the First.

Being Creative

I find lying extraordinarily difficult, not so much from a moral as from a technical viewpoint. I do strongly disapprove of the practice, especially in other people, but it is also very hard to get right. You'd think that as I'm supposed to be a novelist I would find it simple, and in a way I do. I can spin out an unlikely yarn but the snag is I then cannot remember the details. I had a·particularly embarrassing experience in Paris a few years ago. One of my books had just been translated into French and I was supposed to sit on a platform with a panel of literary types and talk about it. This was already sufficiently taxing since my French is at the level which enables me to converse in a desultory way about the pen of my gardener's aunt but little more. I was questioned about various aspects of the plot and found that not only had I forgotten what the book was about but that a number of the characters had also disappeared from my memory. Thus I gave the impression of being either half-witted or an imposter.

The other day I watched a Bette Davis movie in which she played twins. When one of her was drowned the other assumed the role of the deceased. This was irritating enough since the impartial observer could not see how she imagined she could get away with it, but it grew very wearing watching her trying to remember which she was. And then, with this example fresh in my mind, I went and did something similar myself. The phone rang and a foreign voice asked if I was me. The voice belonged to someone I did not wish to talk to so I said I wasn't. The voice asked if I was my daughter and I said no, I was a friend of mine. Then I undertook to pass on a message to myself by which time I had grown incoherent and was losing grasp of my identity. Afterwards I worried a lot, not only about being an awful liar, but about the possible consequences of the deception. Since I had sounded so shifty she might have assumed that I was on the premises for nefarious purposes, burgling the house while the mistress was away. She might have alerted the police. The word 'mistress' conjured up an even more alarming possibility. She might have leapt to the conclusion that since I was away my husband was taking advantage of the situation to entertain a strange woman and his reputation would lie in tatters. This would also make me look a fool, which was even more annoying. I began to wish that I'd never embarked on the pretence but had merely told her, in all honesty, that as far as I was concerned she could go and boil her head. She is a tiresome person who has telephoned other family members several times, trying to enrol me on her side in a conflict of which I know little and care less. It is never pleasant to be impolite but in the end it saves a lot of trouble. I shall try in future to tell the rude truth and shame the devil. This wouldn't work in a political context, politics being the very stuff of lies, but the citizen should at least try to set an example.

So Few Comedians Left in Vale of Tears

I was once watching David Jenkins on TV when I was visited by a sense of *déjà vu*. I have seen this person before, I thought.

There is something of the elderly androgyne in voice and visage; in the grey, fluffy locks, in the *embonpoint*, in the tone which strives to give an impression of academic austerity and is yet irresistibly comic. Who does he remind me of?

Then it came to me. He is a dead ringer for Margaret Rutherford in the role of Miss Marple. The splendid Miss Rutherford was totally miscast in this part but nevertheless added greatly to the gaiety of nations. So too the Bishop of Durham, who is always good for a laugh despite, or possibly because of, the incongruousness of his position. I can hardly bear to contemplate his retirement since we have so few natural comedians in this vale of tears.

The Archbishop of Canterbury is also funny but unfortunately seems to have been overtaken by a sense of prudence, seldom giving utterance to those remarks which once delighted a mirth-starved populace. At one time, to quote Jeffrey Bernard, he only opened his mouth to change feet. Still there are doubtless other Church of England clerics on their way to preferment who will keep the discipline alive.

One, who holds out great promise, has already publicly and categorically denied the existence of God. I have high hopes for him. As indeed I do for several clergymen who give their views on *Thought for the Day*; anodyne, bland and politically correct, they should keep us going for a while yet.

As William Oddie pointed out in a piece in the *Sunday Times* recently, the authors of *Yes, Prime Minister* hit the nail on the head with the observation: 'Theology is a device which makes it possible for unbelievers to stay in the Church of England.' There is also a deep vein of enjoyment to be mined in the debate about the Prince of Wales and his suitability to accede to the position of Head of the Church, and the title of Defensor Fidei which the Pope conferred on Henry VIII before that monarch took up adultery and wife-murder and daylight robbery, and reneged. But then Henry had his funny side. He once wrote a poem (he was young at the time) in which he vowed to be 'eternally true' to some female or other.

It is often said of the Bishop of Durham that he merely voices opinions which are held by the majority of 'thinking Christians', as though for 2000 years a thought had never clouded the purity of the Christian mind. For 'thought' it is now more accurate to read 'doubt', for doubt is currently fashionable and any fat-head can expect to be taken seriously in a climate which fears and despises authority and tradition.

The wafflings of the individual, no matter how unwholesome, must be heard with careful consideration. One of the problems with Dr Jenkins is that I cannot understand his ways of thought since he expresses himself with egregious obfuscation despite being, as I suspect, still anachronistically hooked on logical positivism and 'ordinary language'.

Here he is on the Second Coming of Christ. This is said by him to be 'the picture language of putting together the fact that this world is going to be picked up into God's purposes – and I don't think any of the pictures can be literally interpreted.'

He is, as are many theologians, the equivalent of the paper millionaire, dealing in destructive abstractions which have no relevance to the real world or the plight of humanity; beyond ordinary comprehension and ultimately worthless.

Never mind, the Silly Old Geezer has always had a hallowed place in the hearts of Englishmen and, as long as he holds no real influence, should continue to be treasured.

'A Cross with a Little Man on It?'

It is, I suppose, an urban legend: it obeys the first rule of the game in that it was told to me by a friend of a friend of the friend to whom it happened, and it was told as gospel truth.

One day the third friend went into a jeweller's shop to buy a christening present for her god-child. The assistant, on learning that she wanted a small cross on a chain, enquired, 'Do you want a plain cross or the one with the little man on it?'

The thing about urban legends is that they always reflect some truth about the current state of the mind of society, be they concerned with fear of mad axemen, careless attitudes to mothers-in-law, sexual perversion, or in this case, neo-heathenism. Ignorance of the basic tenets of Christianity is widespread and casual blasphemy is rife. Since the time, some years ago, when the above tale was doing the rounds, crosses have become an item of costume jewellery and the sacred emblem hangs from the pierced, pagan ears of males and females and dangles from the scented necks of party-goers and unbelievers.

The creeping Protestantism which is now afflicting the Church has led to a remarkable loss of the reverence which was once accorded to holy icons, for in a secular society nothing is sacred and rosaries may now be seen hanging over the navels of people in pubs. It is not the vulgarity of all this which concerns me but the lack of awareness and the lemming-like nature of those who blindly follow the fashion.

It is the thoughtless discourtesy which is offensive. People who go about with swastikas stuck on their jumpers or stamped on their heads are undoubtedly more alarming, but you get the feeling that somewhere in the dim recesses of their minds they have some knowledge of what their deplorable emblem signifies. A surprising number of cities, if we are to believe the statistics obtained from questionnaires, demand the Christian rites of baptism, marriage and burial while having only the most tenuous grasp of what these rites mean or entail.

It now seems quite acceptable to make jokes about Christ which if they were made about the Prophet Mohammed, Peace Be Upon Him, would leave the whole of Islam in uproar and seriously deplete our stock of comedians as they were driven into hiding.

Over the Christmas period, twiddling the knob of the radio in search of something not too noisy or fatuous, I overheard a snippet from a comic sketch to the following effect: Joseph comes to the door of the inn and is greeted by the innkeeper. Much mirth is harvested from the extraordinary coincidence of the amazing similarity between the word 'in' and the word 'inn'.

As this joke wears thin, a squawky female voice announces, 'I'm the Virgin Mary and I'm about to have the little baby Jesus and I ain't got nowhere to do it.' Hoots of laughter follow.

I nearly wrote to the BBC to complain, until I was overtaken by apathy as I remembered another humorous radio item I had heard earlier in the year. It was part of a serial about, I think, a priest who ran a boys' football club.

At one stage a lad complained about the tightness of his jock-strap and was told that was nothing compared to what went on in the Garden of Gethsemane. The blasphemous idiocy of this rendered me speechless and I didn't write to the BBC then either. There seemed no point for if the perpetrators were so stupid as to imagine this to be acceptable then they would inevitably be too dumb to understand why anyone should take offence at it.

Now that faith is lost or distorted anything could happen, and while I do not necessarily go along with those who hold that the end of the world is nigh, when I see a crucifix resting in the velvet-upholstered cleavage of an atheist at a party I do feel pessimistic.

Tickled Pink

Funny the things that annoy you. I met a friend the other day who was in a filthy temper because he'd been reading accounts of some people's religious experiences. One person claimed to have seen the face of God in the tempestuous seas and the stormy clouds. 'That was the climatic conditions,' snarled my friend. 'That was the weather forecast. That was Michael Fish, not God.' What really annoyed him was the tacit suggestion that the experience had proved the person to be a better and a more insightful person than the rest of us, and indeed what could be described as spiritual swanking is one of the more repellent aspects of human nature. Television evangelizers in the States do a lot of it, announcing that their unique, personal relationship with the Lord has enabled them to interpret His wishes for mankind. Very often these wishes involve the handing over of large sums of cash to the aforesaid evangelizer, who invariably sports a smile of ineffable self-righteousness. Saints do not carry on like this. Saints, on the whole, when they encounter God, tend to keep rather quiet about it, not bore us all to death with descriptions of conversations of the 'so I said to him, and he said to me' type.

Speaking of death, another friend, the novelist Patrice Chaplin, rang up the other day in a rage because she'd read somewhere that 'only the dead have no more problems'. 'How does *he* know?' she demanded in reference to the author of these words. 'How many dead people does he know? Has he interviewed any? Five maybe? Even one? How does *he* know they haven't got any problems?' We pondered for a while the implications of the paintings of Hieronymus Bosch wherein the dead and the damned are clearly afflicted with problems too various and too painful to enumerate. I shall continue to pray for the Holy Souls in Purgatory in the pious hope that some day someone will do the same for me.

Now I must confess that I wrote that last bit in the serene knowledge that it will make some people cross since many no longer believe in Purgatory or in Hell and get exasperated with us innocents who do. Some of them will write to remonstrate with me on my erroneous beliefs: you can put money on it.

Another group of people who are displeased with me (hopping mad might be closer to the truth) are the proponents of the ordination of women. They write more in anger than in sorrow, demanding to know how I can be so disloyal to my 'sister Christians' as not to back up their ambitions to become priests. Useless to say that my first loyalty is to God and the faith and that I do not feel constrained by my sex to canter unquestioningly along the wilder shores of feminism. One lady says indignantly, 'Surely these women demand the respect and compassion of their sister Christians' (this phrase for some reason gives me the creeps) and I can only respond that while I'm willing to try and work on summoning up the compassion, the respect is beyond my capabilities. I do not believe that women *can* be priests and so find their aims misguided. One of the most basic freedoms is the freedom to choose who or what to respect and to decide for oneself where one's loyalties should lie. The ladies who wish to be priests have chosen their course and I have chosen mine and I'll thank them not to attempt to bully me or to whinge that I'm letting the side down. They have frightened certain bishops into letting them have their say in public but I hope I am made of sterner stuff than some bishops and I won't pay lip-service to heresy.

Just because I'm female doesn't mean I have to agree with whatever daft notion other females come up with, *n'est-ce pas*? Some women are taking up boxing. I wonder if any will write demanding that I identify myself with their aspirations. I would not dream of joining any marginal organization dedicated to denying these ladies their satisfaction, but fur will be the fashion in Hell before I ally myself with them. I hope I haven't plunged anyone into a fit of apoplexy with this view, which I fear is not consonant with either PC or the finer points of feminism, but I'm not sanguine, for it is funny – the things that annoy you.

Five-star Accommodation

It occurred to me the other morning as I was washing my hair that if I were a hotel I should wear on my façade a notice emblazoned with the words, NO CHILDREN. NO DOGS, for while I have loved each and every one of my children very much more than my life this does not mean that I am, as they say, 'fond of children'. Children can be a nuisance when you're trying to tidy the kitchen cupboard and dogs can be a nuisance whatever you're trying to do. My cousin's doberman was contemplating killing me only recently: he pretended he was just playing as he put his paws on my shoulders and gazed down at me, but I saw the gleam in his eye and demanded that my cousin lock him in another room. It took at least half an hour and the better part of a cold, roast chicken before this simple move could be accomplished. Beryl the Jack Russell is a dear little creature but she hates the postman and Jack Ty Coch, who is an essential element in our lives, dealing with pipes, blockages, chimneys etc. – and much time is expended on restraining her from expressing her feelings too overtly.

Then I began to wonder who else would not be welcome on the premises if I were a hotel. Some years ago I'd have said men, for young men also are boisterous and given to knocking things over. At one time I'd have considered only quiet, orderly ladies as suitable guests but now that some ladies have gone mad, I would have to wear, pinned to the brickwork, a notice saying NO WIMMIN.

'I'd have to be a cats' home,' I said gloomily as I examined my conscience later. The friend to whom I addressed this remark thanked me for sharing that with him and asked what I was talking about. I said that (saving his presence) I'd never thought very highly of most men and now I didn't like women either and so was feeling a little isolated and if I were a hotel would undoubtedly go bankrupt. He got me another pint of bitter from the bar.

It is the lugubrious self-righteousness of the feminists that I find so depressing, their insistence on the way they have been 'oppressed' and 'hurt'. The combination of aggressiveness and whining. Before Vatican II I never heard anyone, male or female, fussing that they weren't permitted a role in church affairs, or wailing that the Magisterium wasn't listening to them. We were content to be worshippers and did not attempt nor wish to meddle with the structures of our faith. Now a lot of theologians say patronizingly that that was because we were so 'immature', and all I can say in response is that a lot of theologians talk pitiful tosh and if I were a hotel I'd employ a bouncer to ensure that no theologian came anywhere near me.

It seems that Bishop Budd of Plymouth, thwarted in his efforts to radically alter the cathedral, is now inviting the Catholic Women's Network to present a series of 'women's consciousness-raising' lectures in his diocese during 1994. The heart sinks. I have been to a few of these 'consciousness-raising' events and never found that their preoccupations had the remotest relevance to anything that concerned or interested me. The speakers seemed to be living in another world, agitating themselves about grievances that have no real existence, battling with imaginary monsters and re-creating the past in order to accommodate their distorted view of the present. It was hard to decide whether boredom or embarrassment were uppermost in one's reactions. I have never yet been to a circle-dancing session or one where Wicca and the goddess were invoked and perhaps no one will be astonished if I say that I never will. Nor will I be leaping on the train to Plymouth, where there was a meeting last October to discuss the results of a questionnaire entitled 'Working Together' which had been sent to all the women of the diocese. Dr Elizabeth Stuart, Senior Lecturer in Theology at the College of St Mark and St John, said that 'Apathy amongst women was the biggest problem', and 'exclusive language was oppressive'. Mrs Claire Giarchi, Ecumenical Officer for Devon, said, 'The sense of inferiority of women was apparent in the Church', and 'women are sometimes their own worst enemies and resent other women who take a step forward', while the Revd John Sanders, a deacon from St Austell, said he had 'never realized the depth of hurt that exists among women in the Church'. Since only 3 per cent of the women had responded to the questionnaire one wonders how he got this impression. The speakers were talking garbage and 97 per cent of the women were clearly aware of it. Not all women are as deeply stupid as the CWN appears to think. Praise the Lord. And now I'm closing down the vestibule and going to sleep with the cat on my knee.

PS.   Next week: Why I've Gone Off the Cat.

Save Our Socks

After all, I haven't gone off the cat. I thought I had, but what I had perceived as an act of pure naughtiness on his part turned out to be what is popularly known as a 'cry for help'. He had used a bag of laundry for a most inappropriate purpose and I was planning to sentence him to a long period of detention, or possibly exile, in the Siberian conditions of the outdoor coalhole when we realized he wasn't well. Poor Basil was suffering from cystitis. He was probably also feeling grievously deprived for one of his mistresses had gone back to Los Angeles and the earthquakes. I fear the old-fashioned word 'mistress' makes the blameless Basil sound like a Tory politician but I can't think of another one: he belongs to my daughter who bought him from the pet shop and when she isn't here he is looked after by Nicola, Janet and me. We are all equally devoted to him. Political correctness now decrees that we should speak not of 'pets' but of 'animal-companions', but 'animal-companion shop' sounds silly and Basil could not be more loved if he was called the Grand Panjandrum. He had to spend four days in the care of the vet and it cost us three hundred quid. *Three hundred quid!* For this reason I've gone off the vet. For that sum I could have spent the week in Marrakesh, as I had planned. Oh well, we all have to make sacrifices for our loved ones and foreign travel has its disadvantages.

At the same time as Basil was afflicted our fifth son was struck down by an ailment we fear he might have contracted on his trip down the Amazon. He found it a little strange that whenever anyone enquired as to the welfare of the family I responded – well, I'm all right, but the cat's got cystitis and the boy's got giardia – in that order. But the human sufferer could at least complain in well-expressed Anglo-Saxon while the poor animal could suffer only in silence broken by the occasional heart-rending miaow.

What I like about cats is their independence. They are not importunate as dogs are, constantly begging you to pet them in their need for physical reassurance of your affection and commitment. I greatly dislike being pawed. It is received wisdom at present that we all need to be touched a lot and much fancy foot-work is called for as people bear down on you with their arms outstretched and a look of relentless good will gleaming in their eyes. Princess Diana recommends a great deal of hugging and I heard a vicar on the radio discussing a tragedy and suggesting that everyone should go and hug the bereaved. I have found, in bereavement, such manifestations of pity to be unbearably intrusive. There is only one person, the beloved Xhosa nurse, whose warmth I found comforting because her goodness and sincerity are unassumed and unassuming and not cheaply bestowed.

A friend and I were at Mass the other day and relieved to realize that it wasn't the sort where you're required to shake hands with everyone. Apart from the empty meaninglessness of this tiresome innovation, I have been told by a medical man that it is unhygienic (which is why the Queen wears gloves) and rather more perilous than kissing people. I said I always closed my eyes and pretended I was rapt in prayer and she said that was cheating and she just glared straight ahead and kept her hands clasped on her handbag. It's easier at cocktail parties: you can clutch a glass in one hand and a canapé in the other and merely show your teeth.

Basil does sometimes sit on our heads when we're asleep, or dig his claws in us, but that's because he's hungry or bored, not because he's wallowing in sentimentality. He does not have the misplaced faith in 'humanity' that so many people evince today, but he does put up with us and is usually unfailingly courteous.

A Barking Cat

I read recently that some people were breeding and selling wolf-like dogs and some other people were alarmed. I don't think they need be. My daughter rang from Los Angeles the other day to say that someone had found an abandoned ginger kitten somewhere downtown and brought it home for her. 'Oh,' we twittered, over thousands of miles of sea and landmass, 'a gingery wingery kitteny mitteny. Aaaah.' After some minutes of this I asked what the wulluff thought about it and she said he hadn't seen it yet but she didn't anticipate any problems unless the kitten was overwhelmed by irrational fear. The wulluff is the dog, or rather the wolf, of my fourth son, for in canine terms he goes right back to basics. His mother may have been a dog, although not of Pekingese, terrier, spaniel or Chihuahua sort, but all the rest of his relations are timber wolves. He has golden eyes, a magnificent silvery pelt, powerful muscles and the mild, gently smiling expression common to his kind. Wolves have had a bad press: there are tales from the snowy steppes of brides flung from sledges to assuage the ravenous hunger of the pursuing pack. One wonders why it was always the bride, never the groom or the bridesmaids or the best man or her mother or even a wedding guest: one envisages the wolves trying to chew through layers of satin and tulle, spitting out bits of orange blossom. They would not, of course, usually eat brides, who do not constitute their natural prey, but in times of hardship, a bad winter and famine, they would have little choice. It is obvious that they would rather eat rabbits, grouse or small deer than jettisoned and infuriated brides and I do not think they should be unduly criticized.

The wulluff of my son is referred to by this term because my favourite work of art is the film cartoon starring one Lambsie; the wulluff is his foil and fall guy. I'm on his side, for Lambsie himself is a bit of a twit. People who imagine I have intellectual pretensions are sometimes surprised to learn of my fondness for this entertainment, but our local policeman, Phil the Bill, a person of great sense and kindness, spent much time on his beat calling in at shops to try and buy me a Lambsie video for Christmas. Sadly, he couldn't find one but I bet he put the fear of God into many of the owners of these shops as they hastily positioned themselves in front of the less salubrious items which they purvey to perverts. This gives me a certain satisfaction despite my disappointment.

After a while as I spoke to my daughter, perhaps through an association of ideas, the word 'downtown' registered on my consciousness. 'Whaddaya mean – downtown?' I demanded. 'Downtown is bad. I told you all never to go downtown.' 'Oh *Mum*,' she said wearily, in the way of daughters, going on to explain that they had to go downtown in the course of work for they are in the music business, doing backing sound for (the more salubrious) videos. I said then she'd better take the wolf with her but she said that was impractical. I've hardly slept a wink since.

During one of these wakeful nights I was pondering the Dominicans who have been called Dominicani, 'the Dogs of God', when it occurred to me that the initials of the Catholic Women's Network (CWN) spell the Welsh word which is the plural of dog. I fear that for evermore I shall think of this organization as the Cwn Annwn, which being translated means 'the Hounds of Hell'. Oh dear. I'm sorry, ladies, but one can't help the way one's mind works and it's no good expecting me to be grovellingly polite because it's not in my nature.

Nature, Never a Dull Moment

I've been thinking a lot about nature recently – human nature, Mother Nature, nature red in tooth and claw. I'll begin with the teeth and claws because I've gone off the wulluff. How – I asked my fourth son trustfully – was the ginger kitten getting on with the wolf, back in Los Angeles? There had, he said, been a slight misunderstanding and he had had to prise the party of the first part from the jaws of the second. I expressed myself as much disappointed in the wulluff whom I would not have suspected of such beastliness nor, if I may go so far, of such political incorrectness. Are we not all expected to love one another, and did the wolf not understand that he was supposed to be a New Age icon? Hadn't he seen the movie? My son explained that the animal was an unreconstructed wolf and the movie was far too long and dead boring. Wolves, he said, were used to prey on small furry creatures and I could not but agree for I had just said so myself. There is also a great shortage of brides (who, as I explained last week, get devoured by wolves when times are hard) in LA, not because wolves have eaten them but because most of the men aren't the marrying kind; not the kind that marry ladies anyway. Many of the ladies are very fed up about this but they have only themselves to blame since they have espoused feminism. You can't go round denigrating people and then expect them to marry you.

Then I thought of Mother Nature who, in LA, had been flinging herself about hysterically causing earthquakes, floods and mudslides and much discommoding the human population. Did she not realize that as Earth Mother she was supposed to be evolving, together with all living beings, animals, plants and even gases etc., towards a state of earthly bliss? Was she not up to date on process theology, creation spirituality etc. etc.? Or was she more in accord with the End-Time preachers who tell us that we're all for the chop any minute now? My very best friend in the States had to move from her house into New York City because where she lived old ladies were getting frozen to the pavement and having to be chipped free. Don't, she said, talk to her about Mother Nature.

So then I got round to human nature and had a little think about Pelagius who, as far as I can tell, did not hold with Original Sin and believed we could all progress towards salvation without the assistance of Divine Grace. The evidence is against this. Human nature is markedly flawed in my view. Just consider politicians for a moment if you disagree: these persons present an outward and very visible reminder of our fallen state and offer the rest of us a poor example. Our Saviour redeemed us from the inevitability of Hell but I think we would be unwise to now lie around congratulating ourselves on our native sweetness and presuming we can do without help. We could be in for a nasty surprise. I am presently fond of the woman who I heard on the radio saying that if she had an 'inner child' and was expected to nurture it she only hoped she had an inner au pair girl too to keep the thing under control.

None of us is basically all that nice and the pretence that

we are is fatal. Many theologians when they tell us they are working on development of doctrine fail to add that they are frequently working backwards and hauling up old heresies. Some of them have flopped back into paganism, which makes the intervening centuries seem something of a waste of time. No amount of holding hands, smiling, hopping round in circles, hugging trees or falling over in ecstatic trances will substitute for the painful effort to improve ourselves. Believe me, kids, we're not much and without God's help we're nothing.

Clinically Mediocre

There is an element in the paranoiac personality, so I am told by my friend the psychoanalyst, which cannot tolerate what the paranoiac perceives as 'good' in others – it detracts from his sense of omnipotence. Faced with apparent 'goodness' the paranoiac will attempt to destroy it using whatever means he has at his disposal, be it only denial and mockery. Failing that, he will try and subsume it into himself, obliterating the boundaries – or something like that. Much psychoanalytical theory is now recognized as gobbledygook, especially since the closer look that many people have taken at Freud has revealed him to be unscrupulous, unscientific and a liar. However, there is sense to be found in the more rigorous aspects of the discipline. Neurosis can be defined as a failure to recognize reality, the pretence that the world is different from what it is, followed by the striving to force matters to conform to the neurotic view. Inevitably this causes confusion and eventual chaos and, taken to its logical conclusion, becomes psychosis. When the population starts asking in bewilderment, 'Has everyone gone mad?' it isn't far from the truth.

The current fear and loathing, manifested in many different spheres, of authority and of 'elitism' arises not merely from envy but from this form of insanity – the paranoiac, essentially infantile, detestation of 'otherness'. Take that to its logical conclusion and you reject God. The insistence, prevalent in certain circles, on the immanence of God, the suggestion that He exists only in ourselves and that we need rely *only* on our own consciences to attain to the divine, is, by definition, mad. The 'me' aspect of paranoia presents itself not just in tyranny (Hitler and Stalin are clear examples and so, when you come to think about it, is Freud), but also in democracy which, when it addresses itself to the relentless process of levelling, becomes the tyranny of the mediocre. The majesty, the beauty, the awesomeness of the unknown God are seen as threatening and His wrath is unthinkable. The people turn for comfort to a spurious 'togetherness', emotionalism and blind optimism, with places of worship converted into social centres.

The same sort of thing is happening with the dreaded 're-ordering' and the dangerous (because so easily misunderstood and abused) concept of the initially unexceptionable 'priesthood of the people of God'. Even courtesy, which should consist in a true, God-given respect for the individuality of others, has been distorted into a false and saccharine matiness with the hugs and the handshakes. I am inclined, next time people shake my hand as a sign of their good will and trust, to touch them for a fiver and see what happens.

A bulletin from St Andrew's Cathedral, Glasgow, contains the following: 'For some time we have been thinking about the way in which people come up for communion.' It goes on to fuss about the queuing system and ends: 'Could we also mention that the custom in the cathedral (in common with the vast majority of churches in the diocese) is to receive communion *standing*. Out of courtesy to others you are asked to follow this custom.' Tough luck on anyone whose inclination is to kneel in the presence of his God. There is no

Other but only others who are no different from and certainly no better than ourselves and the existence of a Being whose ways are not our ways is too frightening to acknowledge.

Just Pretend

The Grim Reaper was busy in the soaps in the early spring. He plucked Mark from *The Archers*, Bobby from *Home and Away*, Jim from *Neighbours*, half the cast from *Emmerdale* and Tony from *Brookside*. Not one of these deaths wrung a tear from us. We're not particularly hard-hearted – Nanny starts snivelling at *Madam Butterfly* before the curtain goes up, we both weep copiously over Bette Davis in *Dark Victory* and I have been discovered sobbing in front of *Little House on the Prairie*. Yet the aforementioned deaths left us unmoved except, possibly, to giggles. As Oscar Wilde observed, only a person with a heart of stone could fail to laugh at the death of Little Nell. In the case of *The Archers*, it was perhaps the vicar who preserved us from lachrymosity, for every time the vicar opens his mouth all household activity ceases as we wait for yet another precious utterance of exquisite banality. He talks at the top of his breath and says things like, 'It's such *fun* waiting to get married.' He is the sort of person who, if he had been a girl and at school with one, one would have pulled his plaits till his head came off. At one moment he scaled unprecedented heights of naffness when he was discovered in the church roaring at God because Caroline, his affianced, was lying unconscious. 'Why Caroline?' he was demanding, projecting his voice across the air waves. 'Why not?' we asked when we

85

had recovered our composure. Anyway, she'd be better off dead than united to a person who must cause her unbearable embarrassment on every conceivable occasion.

Our national attitude to death is presently rather peculiar. As the vicar was implying, we seem to imagine that it is something that should only happen to other people – people we don't know. We regard it as an ultimate evil and to be avoided at all costs. There are some in America who arrange to have their bodies (or just their heads) frozen so that they can be resuscitated when the technology's right, and others who have decided that staying alive is only a matter of will-power and they're not going to die – ever. I told somebody that once it was not unusual for certain Catholics to pray for the grace of an early death and he refused to believe me. In a shallow and hedonistic society, where the cult of the individual and the pursuit of happiness are paramount, death seems like a tasteless aberration.

Nor do we now have any idea of how to cope with bereavement. Perhaps those hordes of counsellors help some people but they did nothing for me when my son died, for they tried to tell me I would 'get over it' when all we can do is say, 'Thy will be done', and settle down to live with the loss for the rest of our mortal lives until God in His mercy takes us home. No one was so practical as to warn me of some of the physical effects of grief. After my son's burial I was dry-eyed but overtaken by a desperate fit of choking, and it was only the other day that I read in a Jewish book about mourning that this is quite common. I would have felt less foolish if I'd known that. Nor did anyone tell me about the brief glimpse of glory that can astonish without necessarily consoling you. Nor did they encourage me to do what I wanted, which was to tear my clothes and then sit for hours and days in the presence of the Blessed Sacrament. This was regarded as morbid. Everyone seemed to think that I should be only with other people – who nearly drove me mad.

As I was thinking about death my daughter rang from LA. 'Mum,' she said, 'I've just seen my first murder.' She meant of course in real life, for I believe most children now witness about 30,000 deaths on TV before they reach puberty. A man on the set of a rap video where she was working had lost his temper and shot another one dead. She said she wasn't going to do any more rap videos because not only did people murder people but the very music was an incitement to violence and her conscience wouldn't permit her to go along with it. Don't anyone try and tell me we're not living in a vale of tears – except of course when the vicar turns up to lighten our spirits.

Opportunity Rings

I have always had reservations about the telephone. It can be useful and can save you having to write letters. On the other hand it means you never do write letters and this can make people cross, especially if you forget to telephone them as well. It interrupts your conversations with a masculine lack of consideration and if you ignore it it goes on ringing with female persistence. Often it appears to have gone mad, shrilling away all day like a seagull, sometimes asking you if you would answer a few questions about the service your bank offers you but citing the wrong bank, sometimes maintaining a psychotic silence when you answer it, and occasionally telling you that you have won £6000 in a competition you never entered. When it does this it adopts an upper-class accent with enthusiastic and jolly overtones, congratulating you on your good fortune and adding that you only need hand over £70 in cash to the person who will soon be round on a motor bike. This, it says, will ensure your winnings. When you laugh it actually gets rather offended.

Sometimes it is afflicted with sex mania. It once asked me in a hoarse voice whether there were any electrical points in my bedroom, near my bed. I told it to mind its own business and rang the police. Here it entered into a conspiracy with its fellows and refused to permit me access to the Force. It is often extraordinarily difficult to get through to the police, especially if there's a man in a striped jumper halfway up the drainpipe. Nor does the telephone wish you to talk to the doctor. It considers the doctor far too busy and august a personage to speak to the likes of you. As you lean against the wall, feeling the life ebbing from you, it asks whether you wish to hold.

It is particularly malevolent to those in the throes of passion, managing to indicate that their passion is unrequited. Lovers have been known to sit for hours staring at it and willing it to ring while it sits there, smugly silent. When it does utter it is usually the lover's aunt asking why she hasn't heard from the lover for months and months. The aunt is then offended because the lover's tone is so markedly unaffectionate.

It has just been pointed out to me that the telephone also feels free to be rude in a way that a person in your sitting room would not be. It does not make eye-contact and therefore does not feel compelled to be humane. If it ticks you off you cannot leap on it and beat it up. You can't do much about it at all unless you ruthlessly unplug it from the wall. It is probably worth doing this before you go to bed if you have children in Los Angeles. Otherwise it might wake you at two in the morning to tell you that a green snake in the desert has just jumped in the air about a foot from your daughter's head and given her a bit of a turn. It's hard to get back to sleep after that even if the telephone stays silent. You wonder what secret it's keeping to itself.

Apple is for . . . eh?

I don't know why memory is so unreliable when it comes to questions like what to have for pudding. There are thousands of things to have for pudding but last week I couldn't remember any of them except for apple crumble. That reminded me briefly of baked apple, but for some reason baked apple seemed to present too much of a challenge to the judgement: how long could it stay in the oven before collapsing into stewed apple and do you *have* to shove raisins down the middle of it? I hate raisins, and anyway I didn't know where they were. I don't have too much trouble thinking of serious things for dinner (although I did go through a phase of forgetting everything except shepherd's pie and fried plaice), since there is some scope. As an *aide-mémoire* you can run through all the animals in the Ark, identifying the more palatable, and then remind yourself of the various ways they can end up on the plate. Boiled, baked, fried, fricasséed, etc. You can visualize the fish in the sea and the fowls of the air and you're bound to think of something for dinner. The same goes for vegetables. All you need do is picture the supermarket shelves and potatoes will leap to the mind, cabbage, sprouts, leeks, onions: and when your imagination is warmed up you become adventurous and recall the existence of aubergines, okra, squash and artichokes. There are millions of permutations possible here. Admittedly I only use about half a dozen of them but the mind need never go a complete blank.

Now with puddings it's different. At the moment the only fruit I can think of is the apple. There are still plums about, but I couldn't work out how to make a simple pudding with plums for eleven people (perhaps I should have mentioned earlier that I've been cooking for eleven people). The juice can be a nuisance, rendering the pastry soggy or dripping off the spoon down someone's lace collar. I remembered Queen of Puddings and lemon meringue pie but they are also too much nuisance. The psychological concept of denial comes into play when the memory tries to suggest Spotted Dick or baked sago or jam roll and custard, so in the end it's all down to the apple.

Or, of course, the tinned peach. It may be common but most people have a secret fondness for the tinned peach. Next to the apple orchard we should all keep a cupboardful. I do feel faintly guilty about it, wondering sometimes about a version of the Fall in which Eve is tempted by a tin-opener, but I tell myself this is scrupulosity and invite people to help themselves to loads of cream.

Let Us Consider the Wasp

I've got wasps on my mind – and in my hair and on the butter come to that. There are wasps everywhere, crawling along the floor, creeping over manuscripts, dropping in the sink, buzzing round the light bulbs and occasionally flying in the air, although most of them seem too far gone for that. Visitors keep suggesting that we must have a nest of them somewhere, but I think we merely have a lot of wasps. One year it was flies which took over our house in the country and made our lives a misery.

I read in the paper that we have 6500 species of wasp in this country. 'You must mean in the *world*,' say people when I tell them this but I'm sure it said in this country. I find it hard to believe too. There may well be 6500 wasps in my kitchen alone, but they're all the same sort: little black and yellow striped things that resemble traffic wardens. When they do manage to take off, Basil the cat leaps after them like a ballet dancer, only lighter on his feet. We fear he's going to eat one and do himself a mischief but he doesn't listen to our warnings. My husband, who has never raised his hand in anger to a wasp since he's always thinking about something else, has been stung five times in two days.

This makes me doubtful about something I read in a wildlife magazine. A man wrote that wasps will leave you alone as long as you show no signs of aggression towards them. (This seems to me no truer of wasps than it is of traffic wardens.) He describes an occasion when a wasp sat on his moustache, sharing some jam which had adhered to it. Sated, it then crawled up his face, under his spectacles onto his forehead and flew away. Many people who study wildlife must have nerves of iron, but this is exceptional even among this brave band. Most of us would have been jumping and screaming and flapping the air and demanding of perfect strangers if they could see *it* anywhere. When I think of the frantic scenes I have witnessed at picnics and in beer gardens I am silent in admiration.

Since the human race believes itself to be the peak of creation, it often wonders about the purpose of God in making wasps to annoy it (it feels the same way about traffic wardens), but recent scientific investigation appears to indicate that the wasp carries about it some chemical which, properly extracted and treated, could well prove of benefit to mankind. It's hard to believe they could be useful as you strain them out of the Soave or brush them from the toast and marmalade or shake them from your ankles, but there it is. The Lord's inscrutable ways are indeed hard to understand, but sooner or later the people in the lab will come up with an answer. Even as I write I am tensed nervously lest something should crawl over my foot. Since our wasps are usually no longer capable of flight you have to look down to see them coming. Two of the ones that got my husband had crept up his trouser leg, which put him in an irreligious frame of mind.

I have one other query about wasps: since it is so much easier to say 'wops', why did the English not decide to call them 'wopses'. It is quite difficult to enunciate the word 'wasp' clearly, particularly, I imagine, if you've got one resting in your moustache.

Buzz Off!

We still have a plague of wasps. My husband has swept about two million dead ones into a heap in the dining room and forbidden us to dispose of them: he is curious to know how many more he can add to the collection, and indeed the exercise has a certain morbid interest. It may be the same instinct that leads people to accumulate beer mats or Georgian silver. We are told that the defunct wasps are of no real significance, and that somewhere in the vicinity a Queen Wasp will be settling down to tough it out through the winter. In the spring she will produce another couple of million new wasps. It makes me feel tired. So does the flu. So does TV. I sat through an annoying film the other day, too weary to switch it off. It was all about failure, although it seemed not to be aware of this. In it a young priest, better looking than most priests (indeed, since he was a film star he was better looking than most human beings), grows dissatisfied with his celibate condition and becomes entangled with a rather unpleasant social worker. She appeared ill-mannered and had a very peculiar mouth. I imagine a novelist would describe it as 'mobile' in that it seemed to wriggle around her face a lot, frequently expressing rage or contempt. In one scene she invited the priest in for coffee and the silly fellow accepted. Are they no longer warned about avoiding the occasions of sin? Are they not aware of the heavy eroticism implicit in the word 'coffee'? The usual predictable and unedifying situation followed.

The senior parish priest was represented as acutely boring with a tendency to alcoholism, and when the Cardinal made a brief appearance in a walk-on part he gave the impression of being narrow-minded, if not half-witted. The caricaturing of traditional Catholicism is epidemic, while subjectivism and the soggiest sentimentality are represented as progress. What is going on? You can hardly open a paper or magazine without encountering someone moaning about her repressive Catholic girlhood and boasting that she has flung off the shackles of outdated morality and is now a fully-integrated person. The evidence they give is seldom convincing and I wouldn't want to meet them on a long train journey.

Blasphemy is casually introduced into the many dire sit-coms with which we are afflicted and the producers open a can of hysterical laughter to remind us of how amusing it is. You switch off feeling as though you've been dragged through a garbage bag and brushing off metaphorical tea leaves, festering fish bones and other unmentionable detritus.

But back to our unnaturally handsome young priest wrestling in a desultory way with his inclinations. When he's got his clothes back on he goes to see his mother, who, being an old-fashioned Catholic, is played as a selfish neurotic. Then he prays a bit, but I don't think his mind is on it, then he watches some kiddies scampering about. At some point he worries a trifle about a few parishioners, then he goes off for a holiday with the girl (statutory scene of adult lovers larking about like innocent children in sea/snow/meadow). After a few more moments of uncertainty he settles for breaking his vows and decides to marry her. You just know he's going to regret it. She has wealthy parents, but with one broken marriage behind her, an inability to see any point of view other than her own and her uncertain temper there are sad and stormy times ahead. Besides, there was something about her mouth.

We Shall Sting Them on the Beaches . . .

I hope I've not been boring you with my wasp saga. Anyway it has now, I trust, come to an end. What happened was this: my friend Shelley, with whom I run occasional writing courses, stated that since we had students coming to the house we could not possibly subject them to the dangers presented by wasps. I must, she said decisively, send for the exterminator. So I did. A man arrived with a bag full of something (I did not enquire what) and went on a tour of detection to determine their source. They were, he ascertained, based under the roof. He climbed out of the window and did something (I did not enquire what) and said that was that and we should be troubled no further, so I gave him a cheque. The next day, which was the first day of the course, I was annoyed to find no diminution in the wasp population, although they were already seeming a bit tired. There were three buzzing round the scullery light, one swimming in the sink, about fourteen climbing up the window panes and several fresh corpses lying on the floor, apparently having died from natural causes. I spent much of the lesson, in between discussing the intricacies of characterization, plot and dialogue, leaping up to bash wasps. For this purpose I used a rolled-up copy of the *Spectator* since the heavy quality of the paper makes it a qood weapon. I was constantly alert and thought I had the situation under control when suddenly Shelley, in the midst of a speech on 'The Form of the Modern Novel', remarked in a commendably ladylike fashion, 'Eeek.' A wasp had sneaked silently up and attacked her on the leg. For some reason this caused me to go into hysterics, which was difficult to explain as it appeared unfeeling. It was partly the stoical manner in which she met her misfortune, but mostly it was because of the tragic, artistic and literary aspects of the event. Here we had revenge, self-sacrifice and death (she trod on the wasp). Discussing the drama we decided that the wasps knew that it was Shelley who was the final author of their destruction. They drew lots to see who should take the kamikaze role and avenge his fellows, and resigned themselves to their fate. Shelley and the last wasp were the chosen heroes who engaged in hand-to-hand combat on the ramparts, and Shelley, though wounded, triumphed. I think Alistair MacLean has written books on the same lines. I think Shakespeare wrote plays on the same lines. We spent the evening going over the probable scenario: the last rallying words of the Queen Wasp, the salutations of her doomed warriors, the Intelligence Service which had identified my poor Shelley and the determination with which they sought her out. They were all gone the following day and I'm not sorry although, in a way, you have to admire their grit. I told Shelley consolingly that she should remember that we won, and she said it was all very well for me to talk – I wasn't the one who got stung. So then I had hysterics again but when I recover I'll buy her a medal.

I Vant to Be Alone

I've got flu. Perhaps it was the first symptoms of this disagreeable condition which coloured my views of a person I met recently. She was, on the face of it, a harmless, well-meaning woman but I found her terminally exasperating. She would insist on looking on the bright side. She said she delighted in every aspect of creation. She said she had found herself. She said everything was getting better and better and we should all rejoice. No one in the first throes of influenza sees much to rejoice about, particularly not if she's just been listening to the latest news from the former Yugoslavia as well. When I suggested to my new acquaintance that there were certain grounds for pessimism in the world as it is, she brushed my objections aside and smiled at me pityingly. I am all for a bit of optimism and cheer, but I cannot see the point of the bland proposition that everything in the garden is lovely: not when I see the couch-grass and the thistles swallowing up the petunias before my very eyes. What, I asked, about the increased level of violence in the inner cities? She said she'd personally seen no evidence of it, which is not surprising since she lives in the country. I said almost everyone I knew had been mugged at one time or another, which is almost true (I know a few muggers too), and she said she didn't believe me. I said I thought twice before running down to the off-licence after dark and she implied that I was lacking in faith. I was by now strongly tempted to prove a point by thumping her one, but then she said she was greatly inspired by the teachings of Matthew Fox and I realized she was away with the fairies.

What is worrying about much of the New Age twaddle which has seeped into so many areas of life is that its adherents will not face facts. They say we're entering the Age of Aquarius (although opinions among astrologers vary as to precisely when it did, or will, dawn), and everything is sweetness and light. You only have to travel a little way on the tube to realize that this is not so, but they won't admit it. They still have metaphorical flowers in their hair dating from the dope-crazed sixties, and tell you all you need is love. I avoid them whenever possible, but they crop up everywhere talking about finding themselves. I sympathize with the lady who on hearing someone announce this intention said, 'Yes dear, but are you sure you *want* to?'

Finding the 'inner child' is an even more irritating aspect of this meaningless quest. Here we all are and we are as we are, whatever influences have formed us. I am all for striving for improvement, but see little point in trying to discover some unsuspected and astonishing loveliness concealed in our deepest recesses, crying its eyes out. Even if we imagine we have succeeded in uncovering this hidden aspect, I doubt whether it would cut much ice with our fellows. How would we convince them? How introduce the new, lovable persona? 'You must first love and trust yourself,' say the proponents of this self-affirming doctrine, 'and then everyone will love and trust you.' Sadly this is not so. I, for one, have disliked several people who have claimed to have discovered themselves. So has a family member who shared a flat with one. She had attended consciousness-raising and self-assertiveness classes and persevered in sharing not only the flat but all her insights and resentments. The final straw came when she called a meeting to share her feelings about the way someone had bent her pet teaspoon. She had found herself, which was just as well, since her flatmates all quickly left.

Doctor's Puff

'At this time, Dr Forster says that people should guard against colds, and above all, against the contagion of typhus and other fevers, which are apt to prevail in the early spring. "Smoking tobacco," he observes, "is a very salutary practice in general, as well as being a preventative against infection in particular. The best tobacco is the Turkey, the Persian and what is called Dutch Canaster. Smoking is a custom which should be recommended in the close cottages of the poor, and in great populous towns liable to contagion."' This was written round about 1826 and the message I get from it is that doctors are not to be trusted. Half the time they don't know what they're talking about and the rest of the time they're bullying us. Today we have doctors who are proposing that inveterate smokers should not be treated for illness which they have brought on themselves by persisting in the habit, while other doctors are still suggesting that smoking protects the body from certain afflictions: colitis, schizophrenia and Alzheimer's for instance, if my memory serves me aright. It may not, for I've been cutting down recently and this undoubtedly has a deleterious effect on the concentration.

Many people have already enquired indignantly whether the first group of doctors would refuse to treat people for other self-inflicted ailments. What about the bibulous, the carelessly promiscuous, and those who don't look both ways before crossing the road? I won't ask this question myself, since it leads me down bizarre pathways and makes you think you're going mad. What would happen if midwives turned their backs on those in childbed, maintaining that the silly lady should have known better than to get herself in this condition? The trouble is that doctors tend to forget that they are basically plumbers and they put on airs and play God. I have been told that it was the old Chinese custom to pay the doctor only so long as those of whose health he had charge stayed well. If they fell ill the medical practitioner was either dismissed or put to death. (I won't be able to remember which until I've had another cigarette.) This doesn't seem quite fair either but it helps to put the profession into perspective. It also raises further questions. How did the Chinese doctor, who must have lived in a constant state of nervous tension, prevail upon his patients to abstain from harmful practices? Did he rely on their accepting his advice and strictures or did he follow them round, leaping out of the bamboo thicket and crying, 'Don't *do* that'? I find it hard to picture his state of mind. The modern doctor admittedly has to live with the threat of litigation but will only suffer if he makes a positive error, not if his consulting rooms are full of sick people upon whom he relies to make a living.

It all comes down to the regrettable human urge to lay the blame somewhere. The ailing smoker might sue the tobacco company, saying it's all its fault. The doctor may blame the patient saying it's all his fault. The family of the patient might well say it's all the fault of the doctor for refusing to help and sue *him*. In the end everyone's miserable except the lawyers. Now I've thought of lawyers, I feel more kindly disposed towards doctors. There is something sorely wrong with a society in which recriminations and the acquisition of large sums of money play such a part. Still I don't suppose it was much better in 1826. If everyone had listened to the doctor there must have been a terrible fug.

Speaking of Habits

I've said this before but I'm going to say it again because it's interesting. Puritanism will out. It appears to be as basic an element in human nature as libertinism or a dislike of spiders. If people are permitted licence in one area they will look round for something else on which they can slap prohibitions and wax moralistic.

Smoking is now the favourite social evil. In a recent article I read, the author wrote that he would not patronize a certain restaurant because cigarette girls moved between the tables, plying their wares, and he found smoking the *most* disgusting habit. They should instead, he insisted, sell condoms because they were associated with one of the sources of pleasure that 'don't kill'. Many people still maintain that unbridled sexuality is a harmless and innocent way of passing the time, but they are sadly impractical and out of touch with reality. Sex can be extremely dangerous and bad for the health: people not infrequently murder each other under its influence. Anyway, if I was sitting in a restaurant, I would prefer it if the person at the next table lit up a cigarette rather than indulge his libidinous urges, which would surely cause more disruption than a few puffs of smoke. I am averse to public displays of affection and would much rather watch old movies (where everyone was so busy smoking they barely had time to act), than the new sort where they are all so busy pawing each other they don't have time to smoke. Now, when a couple in a movie kiss, they give the impression of people starting to eat a salt beef sandwich, chewing and gulping. It's enough to put you off your dinner.

I look back with nostalgia to my time in Egypt, where snogging in public was almost a capital offence but everyone smoked, dropping fag ash all over the food and nonchalantly swatting flies as they landed on it. I remember standing at a bus stop in Port Said with an elderly friend who hoicked her veil to one side as she drew on a gasper. Here it is not the women but the food which is covered, virginally wrapped and inviolate until you pay your money and make it your own. All the hygienic regulations have often rendered it virtually tasteless too, but that's another matter. Our puritanism has found expression in protecting food, putting it out of reach of grasping hands or vulgar breath, and in the righteous disapproval of nicotine. This can reach hysterical levels with people removing cigarettes from the lips of perfect strangers. Once, on a train, I delayed a girl from lighting her fag – but only because she was putting the untipped end in her mouth. She was very grateful and will doubtless remember me kindly to the end of her days. In Alexandria our Muslim hostess (who had picked up Western ways), nearly caused a riot by implanting a modest peck on the cheek of my son as we made our departure from an evening's entertainment. All those present waved their cigarettes as they gave vent to their outrage. I feared there would be talk of lapidation but we managed to explain, through the blue fog of the smoke, that such chaste salutations were the custom of our benighted country. They thought it most odd, but made polite allowances for our primitive habits.

Just Get Away

Holidays have always been a rich source of annoyance. Where to go is the first question, then what to do when you get there. If you're going with another person or persons you can argue about these matters quite a lot. Then when you do get there you find it's raining, unless you've gone somewhere where it doesn't often rain in which case it will be too hot. One of you will wish to spend some time viewing the cathedral while others will be unable to think of anything more boring and will whine until they're permitted to go and play the fruit machine, whereupon you yourself go into a sulk. The food won't agree with at least one of you, especially if you're staying in an English boarding-house, and someone is bound to OD on frankfurters and candyfloss because this is a *holiday* after all. Clearly the term 'family holiday' is a classic example of an oxymoron: as is 'good holiday', as in 'what you need is a . . .', or 'pleasant holiday', as in 'thank you so much for the . . .' On the whole the easiest way to relax is to stay at home and make everyone else go away. You know where you are, but the problem with this, at least for the mother, is that she will worry (unless of course she's one of those extraordinary mothers who go off leaving the children alone: she probably wouldn't worry if the toddlers went back-packing round

Essex). If she is divorced from the father of her children she will, in all likelihood, already hold a low opinion of him. Otherwise she wouldn't have divorced him. And if he divorced her she probably hates him more, so when he claims his right to take the children sailing, climbing, skiing or pot-holing she will spend the whole time in a state of hideous anxiety wondering not only whether the children are still sound in mind and limb but also whether their father is bribing his way into their affections by indulging them with promises that they can stay up late and needn't clean their teeth if they're feeling too tired. She won't really enjoy the rest, although Princess Di seems to have had a nice enough time in Bali while Charles looked after the boys at Balmoral. I wonder if she saw that photograph of somebody hanging Harry, a prince of the blood, upside down by his ankles over a loch. I should have wondered whether that person might not be a republican – not to mention merely careless or butter-fingered. I'd have been on the phone rather quickly – 'Tell that idiot to put that child down *at once*.' Someone let Harry drive the Range Rover too. That would have put me off the delicious Indonesian food. I might have caught the next plane home rehearsing a few observations about people who get the children overexcited and render them unmanage-able, a common cause of complaint when Papa has been in charge. Then sometimes Mama takes them away on her own because her husband, separated or not, is too busy with the pressure of work to take time off. I do not think that fathers subject themselves to worry to the same extent that mothers do. No. When mother takes the children away she will still do the worrying but from a different perspective – the underside of the Big Dipper, for instance, while they go up and down. Princess Di on her return from Bali promptly whisked the boys off to Disneyworld: she is either a heroine or bats. I'd rather do time on Dartmoor than go to Orlando. Perhaps that's the answer, a short term in a safe place cut off from the world.

What Angels?

I sometimes have an image of a troop of dark angels, thronging the upper air, going about the world from pole to pole like a bunch of New Age travellers. When they alight en masse they cause huge trouble and resentment. They bring contagion and war and burgeoning bureaucracy; they cause the weather to behave unexpectedly; they afflict our leaders with terminal vanity, deafness and an inability to tell the truth and they sow everywhere the seeds of tax inspectors. Whole nations of previously carefree and peaceable people lose all joy in their youth, all satisfaction in their middle years and totter, stricken by woe, to a pauper's grave. Waste and desolation, despair and a forest of forms to fill in – all these are left in the wake of the itinerant demons.

Sometimes one oversleeps and finds himself cut off from his fellows. Instead of gathering together his belongings and hastening to catch up, he looks round to see what mischief he can wreak unassisted and singles out unsuspecting individuals. One did this only last night. A group of us were sitting down to dinner and talking contentedly when suddenly the chair of one of our number shot out from under him and he cannoned backwards into a waitress who was bearing a vast charger of cheese and biscuits. Gorgonzola, dolcelatte, cheddar were broadcast everywhere, while the victim, a Well-known Personality, writhed in the arms of the astonished waitress. No sooner had order been restored than his immediate neighbour, an Eminent Novelist, suffered the same experience. Her chair was whipped from beneath her and there she lay, flat on the floor. All were agreed that this was no coincidence, no ordinary misfortune, but the work of dark agencies. We sat very still on our chairs, waved away the port and thought of the Four Last Things.

The van of our fifth son was recently backed into by a Spaniard while a demon arranged it so that the son forgot where the horn was, thus preventing him from issuing a warning blast. Then the third son was walked on by a horse: he had been sitting on it until the demon pushed him off, whereupon the son lay in a ditch counting the horse's feet as they flew over his head. Only when the full complement had passed did he consider himself likely to live. He now limps around with the imprint of a large hoof on his thigh. And his wife was struck by lightning. She was talking on the telephone when a blue electric bolt shot between her finger and thumb. Happily only the phone went dead, but it was a further example of devilish ingenuity and spite. Demons like the telephone: when they're not trying to turn it into an instrument of death they use it as a means of annoyance. Mine just rang to remind me that I'd lost someone's manuscript: a piece of information that I could well have done without. I bet the demon's got it in some corner of Hell.

It is fashionable in certain quarters to dismiss the idea of Hell as outmoded and the notion of Satan and his hosts as primitive superstition. Either those who hold this view are singularly blessed or they're not paying attention. There's a stray whiff of sulphur mingling with the pollution in our London air and the sound of the clap of skinny wings. Even as I write the Lord of the Flies has sent one to irritate Basil the cat. I'm not going to do any work today. I'm going to have a word with St Michael the Archangel whose task it is to be our safeguard against the wickedness and snares of the devil. To those rationalists who are smiling pityingly at me I only say 'Beware' and make sure your chairs are firmly anchored to the ground. Don't answer the telephone either. Remember the words of Dorothy Parker when hers rang: 'What fresh hell is this?'

Our Elected Representatives

Politicians have seldom been widely loved or trusted. Shakespeare wrote: 'Get thee glass eyes; / And, like a scurvy politician, seem / To see the things thou dost not.' I'm not certain what he meant by that, but the tone is hostile. I cannot think of any paeans of praise for politicians, except from people making after-dinner speeches when a politician is present, but they do not get into the annals of literature and are usually made either by natural sycophants or by people seeking advancement or advantage – building contracts, motorway café franchises and so on. Politics seems to create an atmosphere of unreality, theatricality; or, to put it more plainly, a favourable environment for the proliferation of lies. We all know what is meant by 'I'm glad you asked me that question.' It's Westminster English for 'I hope you rot in Hell for asking me that question,' but I once heard a politician stonewalling some highly pertinent queries from an interviewer with: 'I'm sure you are aware that I am not in a position to answer points about one specific instance.' Why not? I can't imagine any other situation where you could get away with that device. 'Did you murder your wife?' 'I'm sure you are aware . . .' The interviewer would at least press home the point, but politicians squeal about unfairness when called to account for their more pernicious policies and complain bitterly about unfriendly questioning. They expect not merely huge remuneration and perks but the love and gratitude of the populace and media. It has often been said that no one but a power-crazed lunatic would seek high office with its attendant anxieties, and most politicians, of whatever rank, frequently strike the observer as unbalanced. When caught out in scandalous behaviour (usually sex in the case of Tories and finance on the Left) they are outraged. They almost invariably respond with denials, and then when it becomes clear that they have been lying they wax pathetic and seek sympathy. The implication is that the onerous nature of their duties has forced them into the position in which they find themselves and they deserve nothing but understanding. It seems as though, while constantly thrusting themselves into the limelight, they yet imagine themselves to be invisible when indulging in nefarious activities. It is worrying, though not surprising, that those who govern us are held in contempt by the population. The unholy alliance of politics and high finance has given the country shopping precincts, conifer plantations, rotting motorways and great sweeps of superfluous grain fields. And soon we'll have a Channel Tunnel which will ruin the surrounding coastline and put us all in danger of rabies. Then there's the nuclear industry and pesticides and food additives that the authorities seek to keep us unaware of, and pot-holes in the pavements.

Our leaders refer constantly to the importance of keeping the Party together and are concerned about their own survival, seldom showing as much interest in the country. They are like the blind organisms of a disease which cares nothing for the body in which it breeds and will eventually bring it to destruction. Social engineering is responsible for nearly all our ills, being inimical to the natural development of society.

We do not require our politicians to be lovable (Adolph

Hitler was adored by much of the German nation – and by the Duke of Windsor and a number of English women) but is it too much to wish that they might evince a little common sense? I don't think I'd even mind them lying, a peccadillo seemingly inseparable from politics, if only I felt they were, at any point, in touch with reality.

You Exaggerate, I Believe

I think I may have caught an urban legend at first bounce. Somebody tried the Peruvian rat on me the other day as though it was gospel (the one about the people who smuggle in a puppy dog which sickens, is taken to the vet, and lo and behold . . .). An unlikely story in any circumstances. Years ago I was told by a friend that a friend of her friend's secretary had seen an old lady in the pouring rain, had stopped to give her a lift, noticed that the backs of her hands were covered in hair, evicted her from the car by a ruse, then observed that the old party had left her handbag, took it to the police station and was greatly disconcerted, to put it no higher, to discover that it contained nothing but a meat cleaver. I believed that one for two days until several more people told me that it had happened to a friend of their friend's daughter/mother/sister. It is the number of people who stand between the story-teller and the story that I think is significant and the surest proof that what you are hearing is one of those curious fairytales that seem suddenly to occur spontaneously all over the country. It is never 'I was in Spain with my mother-in-law when she died so we stuck her in a rug on the roof of the car and it was stolen . . .' It is always a friend of a business acquaintance of a friend. Two or more removes.

The following story was told to me by a friend who had heard it from the sister of the WPC who had been called by anxious neighbours to investigate an incident.

It was late afternoon and the peace of the neighbourhood was disturbed by muffled yells and crashes emanating from a flat. After a while and some consultation the neighbours sent for the police. When the police arrived everyone crowded round to peer over their shoulders to see what was going on. There on the bed was a lady, wrists and ankles lashed securely to the bedposts (already you can see that this is a dubious tale since most people now sleep on futons or sofa-beds and have no useful bedposts). From the locked wardrobe there came a desperate pounding. The police unlocked the wardrobe doors and out stepped a gentleman dressed as Batman. He was not, as the neighbours were quick to notice, the husband of the lady. He was a friend and the idea behind the whole exercise was that they should enact a sort of knight-on-a-white-horse fantasy: she bound and helpless and he – the hero – perched aloft the wardrobe whence he would leap gracefully to her rescue. Everything went wrong when the top of the wardrobe gave way (you can't trust this modern furniture: it's all made from chipboard) and Batman crashed down among the dresses and suits and coat-hangers to find himself securely imprisoned. A nightmare scenario, you will agree, but do you believe it? I don't. I don't believe that if Batman was heavy enough to fall into the wardrobe he wouldn't be strong enough to break his way out. And if he was prepared to jump off the top of it surely he would be sufficiently lissom to claw his way up, emerging triumphant like the Demon King in a pantomime. The whole thing is pure pantomime. How interesting that even with *Neighbours* and *EastEnders* and all the entertainment offered by TV we still seem to have the ability and the need to create our own folk-tales.

Look Fair to Me

I have been reading a *Miscellany of Useful and Entertaining Tracts*. One of them concerns an eighteenth-century Frenchman, Lesurques, who had the misfortune to resemble a highwayman, one Dubosq. This man, with some partners in crime, had ambushed the Lyons Mail, nearly severed the head of the Lyons Courier and also murdered the postillion. In between times they had visited various inns and hostelries, having a spur mended and returning for a sabre which they had forgotten, as though it were a mere umbrella. It is a confused tale and the witnesses, perhaps understandably, were all a little bewildered. Nevertheless they swore that Lesurques was one of the broken-spurred company, and he was brought to trial and convicted. At this point the mistress of one of the real villains 'called aloud in a violent state of excitement from the midst of the crowd' that Lesurques was innocent. 'The witnesses had mistaken him for Dubosq, to whom he bore an extraordinary resemblance.' Several people had insisted that Lesurques had been with them at the time of the murder, but one, in a fit of overenthusiasm, had clumsily (and unnecessarily) altered a date in his diary in order to corroborate his testimony. 'This circumstance produced the most unfavourable effect on the Judges', and in the manner of judges with the bit between their teeth, they disregarded the evidence of the wretched man's innocence and announced that the law must take its course. On being approached by the Directory with a message requesting a reprieve, the legislative body remarked that 'as all legal forms had been fulfilled, a single case ought not to cause an infraction of forms previously settled; and that to annul on such grounds the sentence legally pronounced by a jury, would subvert all ideas of justice and equality before the law!' The compiler of this tract went into incredulous italics as he quoted this, ending with a horrified exclamation mark, and I don't blame him.

Many contemporary journalists have behaved similarly, reporting the observation of one of our learned judges pontificating on one of our own glaring miscarriages of justice. Sometimes the law seems to be enclosed entirely within itself and neglectful of the immaterial and inconvenient truth of the matter.

Nor is one reassured by the proposed 'reforms' in the law presently under discussion. Juries are not infallible – but nor, on the evidence, are judges. Sometimes one feels that so arbitrary and uncertain are the processes of justice that one might as well elect for trial by ducking-stool.

After Lesurques was decapitated the jury 'expressed their regret at having given credit to the witnesses from Mongeron and Lieursant and Citizen Dambenton, the Juge de Paix . . .' etc. But, by then, it was really a bit late.

Plus ça change, plus c'est la même chose.

Dull Days

Tedium vitae, accidie, ennui, or as we put it in our own part of contemporary Europe – bored stiff: an unpleasant condition whether due to some disorder or deficiency in the personality or to prevailing circumstances. I am not alone in finding myself short of that vitality, that bright-eyed interest in what is going on around us which makes life endurable. I know several people who presently feel the lack of a certain spark. Some put it down to lead in the atmosphere, some to the lead in their teeth, and rightly it is described as a leaden sensation. Can it be due to the wearisome nature of the Maastricht debate, the dreary personae of our leaders and the transparency of the lies they tell? Is it due in part to the miserable state of publishing and the scarcity of good new books? Or is it just the weather?

Even the birds seem bored: they walk in the garden in a heavy, desultory sort of way and get killed by the cat – when he can be bothered to exert himself, for even he is yawning more than usual. I think they may be hoping for some excitement. Anything to interrupt the remorseless procession of dull days. We have not ourselves yet gone to the lengths of considering dicing with death to relieve the tedium. We thought of going abroad, but in the places we wanted to go you run the risk of getting shot – the Valley of the Kings, for

120

instance – and in the supposedly safe places homogeneity reigns and you are likely to find yourself confronted by yet another McDonald's. It is most dispiriting.

Nor does the current state of religion offer much diversion. Cant and kindergarten activities have in many churches replaced truth and dignity, and the suggestion that we should all clap our hands for Jesus induces in me only the urge to retire to the pub and ingest a cleansing draught of whisky. New Age 'thought' (I use the term loosely) advises that we all hold within ourselves as well as the 'inner child', the Goddess, truth and beauty, male and female, healer and healed and goodness knows what else. Chemical Weddings, Hidden Suns, Sacred Mountains are all mentioned in New Age outpourings and none of it is remotely interesting. On the contrary: it is meaningless, futile, depressing and ultimately boring, as magic and witchcraft have always been. The fact that such pointless and *vieux jeu* activities as circle-dancing, cairn-building, hopping around with hard-boiled eggs and balls of red yarn have percolated into certain 'Christian' groups beggars belief, but there it is. I think I have now located the source of my own unease. I've been reading about these matters in the course of research and it has lowered my resistance to despair. Despair and boredom are close cousins. The next time anyone tries to share with me the beautiful message she has just had channelled from a dead Red Indian I shall stick my fingers in my ears.

Stuff, Nonsense, and More Stuff

Why do we do it? Why do we encumber ourselves with possessions? We are born with nothing yet the moment we emerge into the light of day people start pressing *things* upon us. Before the neonate knows where it is, it is the owner of bears and frilly frocks and books about bears and a christening mug. As time passes it gets birthday presents and Christmas presents and its room is a mess before it's old enough to articulate its feelings on the matter. By then the human being has taken it for granted that the possession of things is an essential element of human existence and as he grows up he, or perhaps more frequently she, goes shopping and buys more. I sometimes wonder if anyone in what is known as the developed world can open a cupboard without being flattened by a torrent of things already falling prey to moth and rust and the various forms of corruption consequent upon the second law of thermodynamics. (I think that's the one I mean.) I've doubtless got a book about it somewhere; probably at the back of a cupboard behind the broken flat iron and the platform-soled shoes and the incomplete jigsaw.

In the old days, so I am told, the nun could call nothing her own except for her bed and her dentures, and I dare say her toothbrush if she had a full set of natural gnashers. No wonder they used to look so carefree. I sometimes read about people who own four houses, a castle in Spain and a yacht, all of them fully kitted out with the articles considered necessary to everyday life: Ming vases and Chippendale dining chairs, etc. Do they never have a moment's worry as they picture the butler draining the contents of the cellar and dropping the Rockingham dinner service? Or an unauthorized visitor painting a moustache on the Rubens? The responsibility of owning treasures must be awesome but perhaps the *haute monde* are too blasé to worry about such eventualities. Perhaps they put their faith in the insurance.

I once wrote an article advising people that I didn't want any more presents and I would prefer them to take something away. A burglar promptly arrived and obligingly lifted the TV. It was too late to explain that I didn't mean *that*. I meant the bath salts and the three sets of gloves and muffler and the illustrated book of Indonesian cookery and the golfing umbrella and the machine for making pasta. He would have been welcome to three or four outworn anoraks and overcoats, a few hundred odd socks and the buckled pushchair, but he had to go and take the telly. I hope he already had a cupboardful and his wife left him.

You can't even go to your grave without somebody trying to persuade your grieving relations that you won't be content without a smart coffin with brass handles and knobs on, your face made-up and a natty shroud. What is wrong with us? Still, we're not as bad as some much-admired older cultures in this respect. We don't insist on slaughtering the hired help and the household pets to accompany us on our journey to the nether world: we won't demand to be buried with the fishforks and a sufficiency of sandwiches and Scotch to sustain us through eternity. Even the most ardent member of the consumer society has to accept, albeit reluctantly, that you can't take it with you. I only wish I'd understood earlier that

most of it you don't need even in the here and now. When I
think of the junk under the stairs I wish I was a mendicant
friar. Don't tell me to give it away. Nobody, I assure you,
would want it unless they were nuts.

Put That Heart *Down*!

'Don't,' advised Kipling, 'give your heart to a dog to tear.'
Such a sensible recommendation and so often disregarded. I
once read a book in which a child had to go and live with her
aunts, leaving behind both the servant who had brought her
up and her cat. The servant remarked aggrievedly that as far
as she could see the child was more upset at being parted
from the cat than from herself. The child, astonished, wondered how there could be any doubt about it. Of course she
was going to miss the cat most. Happily she had the sense not
to say so out loud. Many people get cross when they suspect
others of preferring animals to human beings, especially if
they happen to be the human being in question. I must
confess that I like some animals better than some people: I'd
rather go for a walk with Beryl the dog than with a disgruntled
philosopher for instance. She might make a nuisance of herself
by chasing rabbits but she wouldn't attempt to convince me
that belief in God was irrational.

I must also admit to entertaining the possibility that
animals have souls and might well go to Heaven: in my wilder
moments I even toy with the notion of reincarnation, suspecting that Basil the cat was a mongoose last time and will be a
philosopher, or possibly a violinist, next. He likes killing
snake-like strips of plastic, has a donnish sense of fun, always

repeating his jokes, and evinces a marked interest in elastic bands and the strings of stringed instruments. I know people with less personality.

However, at the moment, I am more concerned about our old cat, one Puss. She is fourteen, only possesses one kidney and is not at all well. The vet has given it as his opinion that she is dehydrated and has put her into hospital, which will undoubtedly cost a lot of money. She must be well into at least her eighth life by now and I'm having great difficulty trying to decide whether I'm more concerned about the expense or her quality of life should she rally. The examination of conscience can be very taxing in cases like this. I'm almost sure I'm more worried by the possibility that she might be miserable but one can never be certain. The sorrow when people or cats whom you love, die, is always exacerbated by the guilt you feel about the time you told them their frock didn't suit them, or the occasion you threw them out of the kitchen for dipping their whiskers in the trifle. I hope with all my heart that we will have time – indeed eternity – in which to apologize.

Luckily there are no small children around at the moment, so if I have to tell the cat that 'the moment has come to be brave' (as the executioner used to remark to the condemned man as he wound up the guillotine), I will not have to confront a row of reproachful faces and brimming eyes. I found that the only films I had to forbid my children to watch (except, of course, for nearly all the latest ones – but that was on different grounds) were those involving animals, since something sad always happened, and children who can contemplate the death of Sydney Carton with equanimity cannot sleep for sorrow because Lassie had a thorn in her paw.

Bouquet of Broccoli

Where have all the flowers gone? This is not a rhetorical question. I want to know. There is a horrid sameness about municipal gardens and parks and hanging baskets: we are everywhere faced with lobelia, alyssum, salvias, pelargoniums, calceolaria, overweight pansies and odourless roses. Somebody bought me some carnations the other day and every time anyone went near them they said, 'Good heavens, they actually *smell*.' (Dr Johnson would have said, 'No madam, you smell, I stink . . .' or something on those lines, but he wasn't there.) They looked as boring as most bought flowers do but they had *something* going for them.

I am seldom as delighted as I should be on those festive occasions when large bouquets, shrouded in transparent paper arrive: mindless groupings of the same old blooms which have to be separated before they look anything but familiarly messy. I'd rather have a bottle of Scotch or a bunch of dog daisies shoved in a jam jar, for I deeply detest flower 'arrangements'; carnations and chrysanthemums and lilies with a spray of gypsophila and a strand of cypress or privet gripped round the stems with a big plastic bow: all strangers to each other by virtue of origin or season and forced into unnatural proximity. We stand ankle-deep in fallen petals and scissored stalks, sorting them into different jugs and vases and two days later they're all dead. When roses in bud arrive they seldom mature but droop their infant heads and fade away without opening: a sad reminder of mortality, the futility of earthly endeavour and the ineptitude of market gardeners. An illustration of the human urge to control by denying diversity; the potentially fatal move to homogeneity, since the fewer the species the greater the prospect of extinction. Where are all the old-fashioned, blowsy, scented roses and all the pretty things that used to grow in cottage gardens? Gone, to make way for the lobelia, alyssum, salvias, etc. together with those ugly dwarf conifers and banks of erica beloved of suburbia. It is worrying that nearly all market gardens sell the same plants and alarming that people unquestioningly buy them and cause their gardens and hanging baskets to look identical to the garden next door.

Our garden doesn't. It is overgrown and well out of control. This is not a matter for pride but it does remind one of the power of nature left to itself. The ash which seeded itself is now seeding other little ashes, and looking down from the top windows all we see is a forest canopy. Our answer to the depletion of the rain forest, except that the garden is only the size of the average kitchen. People have to hack their way through ivy, virginia creeper, honeysuckle and jasmine to get to the door and put the key in the lock. In the backyard (which is the size of the average lavatory) there grows a huge magnolia which I planted myself when it was small enough to put in a jug. I never imagined or intended that it should grow as high as the house. I wonder what it's doing to the drains. Clearly nature must be controlled if it is not to overwhelm us and I'm still annoyed with the ivy which crept under the window frame and tore the lining from the curtains, but I'd rather that than live surrounded by the tame and scentless sameness of the bedding plant. It's quite exciting to live just a little dangerously.

Wake Me at the Interval

I have a pitifully low boredom threshold. Yes, yes I know
only very boring people are easily bored. A friend, whose
mother used to tell her so, found that the remark rather
lessened the warmth of this closest of all relationships.
There's nothing you can do about it: if you're easily bored,
you're easily bored, and you have to be extremely careful
about where you go and who you mix with. It's not a
condition which is readily disguised: from straying attention
and the glassy look in the eye to apparent catatonia, the state
makes itself obvious and, almost invariably, causes offence.
The simplest remedy is to take no chances and avoid the
occasions of boredom. For instance, never dine out with
people either in restaurants or in their houses unless you
know them so well they won't mind if you bring a book with
you. Something to read is the one absolutely basic essential
for those prone to *ennui* and the serious sufferer makes sure
that all her garments have capacious pockets where she can
secrete, at least, a magazine or newspaper. I cannot settle
down in front of the TV unless I have the channel control
gripped firmly in one hand and a novel in the other. This
tendency makes theatre-going difficult, since you cannot
change channels. There is a device consisting of a kind of
plastic envelope, wherein you slip a book, with a little torch

affixed to the top: in theory this illuminates the page but in practice it doesn't. Besides, even perfect strangers take offence if they see you reading while they are enthralled by the play. I usually doze. One of our sons, who I fear takes after me to a remarkable extent, goes into profound slumber and snores. He ruined a beautiful relationship by doing this during a performance in which his then best-beloved was acting her socks off.

Only the other day I inadvertently let myself in for an evening at the theatre by saying that I would be enchanted to see a Russian play. The person to whom I said it responded by assuring me that there were still one or two tickets available at the box office. As he was playing a significant role in the production I had no option but to hand over a large sum of money and take my seat. The next time I saw him, from my place in the auditorium, he was clad only in a thin layer of mud. He was excellent in the part and has a notably resonant voice, so while not looking too closely I listened carefully until he was murdered, whereupon I went to sleep.

I have to confess and will, naturally, do so in the course of my Easter duties, that my attention also wanders in church unless I am present at a Tridentine Mass where you have to keep your wits about you. The assumption that the various new forms of Mass will give the worshipper a greater sense of participation is, in my case, mistaken. I spend my time speculating on the motives of those who deprived us of the beauties of the liturgy and endeavouring to get into a position where I can avoid shaking hands with anyone. If I ever again visit a certain church where innovation is rife I can see myself wondering how long it will be before the priest appears clad only in a thin layer of mud on the grounds that 'that was the way it was done in the early Church'. I would not be unduly surprised in the light of other startling developments I have witnessed, and, sadly, even astonishment is not a sufficient specific against boredom.

The Price of Fish

Agoraphobia, as is well known to us Classical scholars, means literally 'fear of the market place'. And I am suffering from it, literally. On the other hand, if I'm to be totally honest, it was not until the other day so much fear as boredom, idleness and a disinclination ever to go shopping again. Shopping is tiring, annoying and alarmingly expensive. How often does one come home, dump one's carrier bags on the kitchen floor and remark incredulously, 'You won't *believe* what I've just paid for fish': especially if one has splashed out, as it were, on monkfish, which used to be the sort you bought because it was cheap. In all probability the shopper, if she is of an age to remember, will go on to moan that if anyone had told her twenty years ago that before she died she'd find herself paying the equivalent of a couple of quid in old money for a loaf she'd have thought him mad. If she has been to the supermarket she will be suffering from a touch of super-agoraphobia and will be snarling that she spent hours at the check-out till because the price ticket had dropped off the avocado of the person in front of her, and operations had come to a standstill while runners were located and dispatched to ascertain the precise value of the article. Sometimes she will have had her pocket picked, been run over by a trolley or abused by the person behind her in the queue because the price ticket has dropped off her own avocado.

The Price of Fish

Our market place was once a civilized little area with proper shops and shopkeepers. These have all now disappeared and in their place are bistros, sandwich bars and outlets for shoes, shell-suits and horror comics. The fruit and vegetable stalls remain but unfortunately the street where they stand is subject to a Siberian draught and, as there are no longer any little grocers' shops to dash into and warm up while discussing the relative merits of various types of rice, the inclination is to speed through, making one's purchases without due care and attention. One comes home to find that one has forgotten the cauliflower, which is what one had gone out for.

This is all trying enough, even leaving out of consideration the extraordinary filth and detritus of the pavements and the holes in the road, but the other day a bomb went off in the High Street. None of us was shopping at the time but a friend was in the nearby alternative medicine centre, stuck full of acupuncture needles, and ever since has been speechless, not with shock, but indignation. We all heard the bang and somebody said, 'That's a bomb.' 'So it is,' the rest of us agreed, and what is remarkable is that none of us was unduly astonished, having grown accustomed to these alarms. This is what annoyed my friend with the needles: she, like the rest of us, has become more or less used to the extraordinary cost of bread and butter, the corruption and disorder of the city, the cynical insistence of our leaders that everything is OK really and getting better all the time, but what enrages her – and who can blame her since she might have been blown to bits – is the apathy with which the citizenry treats such events. The market place was briefly closed off and I was upset because I couldn't get to the off-licence and we were expecting visitors who would be expecting drinks, but it was only later that I realized that we now have real cause for agoraphobia – not just the fear of penury and the wind-chill factor, but the possibility of injury and death. I suppose it puts the price of fish into perspective.

Sitting on the Fence

The human urge to take sides can prove frustrating when you can't decide which side of the fence you'd rather be on. It seems craven just to sit on it, and is also boring, but choice can be difficult.

Take the Boat Race. You don't really care in the least who wins or even if both Oxford and Cambridge slowly founder, but you feel you should. It's simpler with tennis: you just hope the loud-mouth loses, but if you have no strong territorial instinct it's hard to get excited about the World Cup.

I've got a problem with hunting, having always found it impossible to warm to people who cavort about the country-side flattening the crops in pursuit of the poor little furry fox. I feel like this about the fox until I'm given evidence of what he did in the hen coop whereupon I find myself on the side of the chicken. You are doubtless familiar with the problem. I never had any sympathy with the master of the hunt, even when they broke their collarbones or worse, but neither can I identify with hunt saboteurs, who seem a most unamiable crew.

You get the impression they don't love foxes as much as they hate people and are using Reynard as an excuse to haul the aforesaid people off their high horses. Highly unedifying scenes result with much laying about of horse whips and evil language while the fox is probably brushing the feathers off his whiskers.

Round our way they hunt foxes on foot with terriers and guns, a practice profoundly scorned by the horse-bound, who call it vulpicide and can hardly bear to contemplate it. Nor can we, but for different reasons. Hunters are unmoved by the spectacle of dogs running round with bits of fox dangling from their dripping jaws but it puts the ordinary citizen off his lunch. Happily I was absent on the particular day of carnage I have in mind but family members were upset.

It seems that foxes had made unacceptable inroads into Sir's pheasants and steps had to be taken. If the foxes had only been as cunning as they're said to be they'd have eaten the rabbits and won themselves a round of applause but they had to go and annoy the gamekeeper and bring retribution upon themselves. I believe the scene was like Armageddon out in the garden, ankle deep in blood. Allowing for the exaggeration so often generated by righteous indignation it still sounds like something with Arnold Schwarzenegger in it. How trying are these moral dilemmas.

It is said that the baby foxes also tear up baby lambs, a habit which cannot be condoned, but then you think of baby foxes with their wide innocent eyes and their playful ways and have to remind yourself of what they say of so many murderers – 'He was such a charming, mild-mannered little man, you wouldn't have thought he'd hurt a fly.'

I have probably spent many evenings in the pub with the hunters home from the hill, when they've washed off the gore and combed the twigs out of their hair, and found them pleasing company, better than being out with the shy wild things in their rank habitations on the inhospitable mountainside.

Sitting on the Fence

I *would* sit on the fence, only it's hung with dead foxes and
other creatures, put there by the gamekeeper to frighten their
fellows. They make poor companions.

Double Jeopardy

When I was last on my way to Confession I was kind to two Jehovah's Witnesses. They were standing on someone else's doorstep and I advised them not to go and stand on mine: there are two doors at the front of the house which leads people to suppose that there are two households therein, so, once past the gate, they knock on the top one and then plod down the steps and knock on the bottom one. Should they be cult members this is most unwise, for the head of the family, having told them once not to be so stupid and to stop wasting his time, gleefully flies downstairs and tells them again. It's enough to shake anyone's faith. I myself have a tendency not to let them, or anyone in. We have a technological arrangement whereby the gate can only be opened from inside the house: there is one of these phones whereby you enquire who's there, but I seldom use it since once they know you're at home it seems rude to refuse them entry. What I do is to drop on all fours and peer through the bottom of the sitting-room window to see if by any chance it's my very best friend and not someone demanding astronomical sums for a tea towel or trying to persuade me to read *The Watchtower* or impel me to join the followers of Joseph Smith. (I must remember to go and stand at the gate, get someone else to crawl to the window on her hands and knees and check

138

whether I can see her. It would not be dignified if one was visible to the caller.)

Once upon a time the callers might have been the Christian Brothers but the clergy seem to have given up on missionary activity round here. I do miss them. They used to talk about Hell, and were most interesting. Nobody seems to talk about Hell any more, or even sin. When I got to the confessional and admitted I had fallen short of the Ideal, the priest confessed himself concerned about my low level of self-esteem. Has everybody gone mad?

Still, one of our regular callers is an Upholder of the Law and always welcome. He is our homebeat policeman and pops in several times a week for a cup of tea and slice of cake, should there happen to be one lying around. The thing on his shoulder which jabbers away like a parrot is somewhat disconcerting but you get used to it after a while. The only real snag about having a uniformed police officer frequently ringing at your gate is that it makes the neighbours wonder what you've been up to. On the other hand it must discourage the burglar who used to stroll in and help himself to household articles with distressing regularity. I do rather miss the knife-grinder who was still calling at the door about ten years ago. He was a thief too but he had a wooden leg and a raffish air. He was lousy at grinding knives but his presence added a certain historical tone to the district. There was also a chair-mender who used to re-cane chairs with the minimum of effort and the minimum of cane so that he was always in demand as yet another person went through the seat. No, on the whole callers at the door are not what they used to be. Market researchers are very dull by comparison, and no real tradesmen bother to schlep their wares about any more. I'm just going to add a warning to anyone who might be planning to call. Two pigeons are building a nest in the tree next door and their habits are deplorable. If you intend spending any time standing at the gate while we scrutinize you through the fronds of ivy, make sure that you have a stout umbrella.

No More Excuses, But . . .

Ursine garlic, or as the latin has it, *allium ursinum*, is dedicated to St Leo IX, Pope. I didn't know that until the other day when I had no excuse for not sitting down and writing. Once I heard of a woman who actually enjoyed writing. She got up early and carried her cup of coffee with her to her desk where she sat down gladly and took up her pen. Everyone else hates it. Everyone else has four cups of coffee and a banana sandwich and a cold frankfurter before they face that sheet of deadly white paper. They let the cat out and then they let him in again, they telephone their aunt to enquire about her sciatica, they water the geranium and then remember they need batteries for their radio so they go to the shop. The person you see in the street stopping passers-by to talk about the weather is probably in the throes of writing a book.

I don't know whether it's easier working on a word-processor. There are those who say the screen is less daunting than the blank paper and the words already appear to possess some authority as they pop up in front of your eyes, but when I see a screen I expect it to be showing *Neighbours* or *The Simpsons* or something more amusing than my own words. As soon as I find myself trapped in a room with a sheet of blank paper (having tended the cat and the pot plant etc. and run out of excuses) I pick up a book to see what some other poor

141

idiot has made of the business. That's how I know about ursine garlic and Pope Leo IX. What's more I also know that *narcissus orientalis albus* is dedicated to St Anselm. This intelligence and much, much more is contained in an early Victorian tome called *The Every-Day Book*, a mine of dated, useless and perfectly fascinating information: it runs to 1718 pages with index and illustrations and was compiled by a person who clearly did not detest writing.

When you come to think about it, few of the Victorians can have detested writing since they did so much of it: those who weren't writing books in three volumes were writing letters and keeping diaries and shooting off *billets-doux* in all directions. Hating writing must be a modern phenomenon. The author of the work under consideration loved it and could barely restrain himself. He takes nearly six columns to describe the prowess of one Madame Mara (born 1750). She started off playing the violin but on the advice of English ladies who 'disliked a female fiddler' took up singing. She could go up and down the scale, while leaping all over the stage, on account of her 'power of chest', and possessed 'majesty, simplicity, tenderness, pathos and elegance'. I don't know why but I don't warm to her.

I also learn that the Italians had a saying as follows: 'of the hundred requisites to make a singer, he who has a fine voice has ninety-nine'. Fancy that. Then I read a long-winded anecdote about rooks falling out of trees which was chiefly interesting because it uses the figure of speech 'hopp'd the twig' for dying, which I thought was recently invented. Then I was reminded that Romulus slew Remus in 753 BC because he'd 'ridiculed the slenderness' of the nice new walls of Rome, and Alexander the Great died of drink at the age of thirty-two. There are accounts of bear- and lion-baiting which I skipped, and a number of disparaging descriptions of Romish practices. This causes one to wonder why the author insists on telling us which plant is dedicated to which saint. St Cajetan is lumbered with *amaranthus hypochondriacus*. Now I have to forget all that and start assembling yet another book. How absurd life is.

Please, Exclude Me

The English publication of the new Catechism was held up while everyone fussed away about whether or not to use 'inclusive language', 'he/she/their'. What a waste of time.

When I read the word 'he' in a general discussion of the human condition I know what it implies. I do not immediately visualize a hairy satyr prancing all over the page, but take the term as anonymous and androgynous. If, however, I read a work in which the author has chosen rather to employ the word 'she' I get an instant vision of an entirely personal creature, as often as not of a bosomy bossy-boots in twin-set and pearls. It's very distracting. My husband, who is by trade a publisher, was recently editing a work of philosophy by a lady who had elected to use this grammatical device: he altered nothing until he came to a phrase on the following lines: 'She turned to her assailant and kicked him.' My husband blandly altered 'him' to 'her'.

When I was a little girl the women of my acquaintance took the view of the lady in Mrs Gaskell's *Cranford* who had no doubts about the equality of the sexes: she knew that women were the superior sex and saw no point in arguing about it. I have in my time been annoyed by men who, laying claim to greater virtue, have suggested that the members of their own sex are magnanimous, generous and loyal whereas the female of the species is jealous, mean and given to malicious gossip. 'Invert that,' I say truculently, 'and you'll be getting close.'

This is one of the reasons why I have no desire to join any men's club, having noticed that, with the decline of the public school ethos, masculine gatherings are characterized by competitiveness, envy and pettiness. Men never used to throw themselves round in a tantrum if they lost a game, or sink their teeth in a member of the opposing team when no one was looking. They had an ideal of sportsmanship and most of them tried to live up to it.

Women of course have never needed this ideal since, until recently, they had enough sense to know what was and what was not done in a social context and behaved with restraint because it made life simpler. Then some of them got bees in their bonnets about this wretched 'equality', which is in any case a pretty meaningless concept, and decided, for some reason which I'll never fathom, that men were having a better time of it and they were going, not only to join them but wherever possible oust them from their positions. There's been nothing but trouble ever since.

Men are perfectly all right in their way, when they remember how to behave, but I can't imagine why a woman should wish to resemble one.

Militant feminists make me think of Wellington's reflection on regarding his troops – that he didn't know what they'd do to the enemy, but by gad they frightened him. Rabid feminists frighten everybody, particularly bishops, and make the men bad-tempered and difficult.

The decline in masculine standards is co-eval with feminism and arises from the same cause: the concept of 'Me First'. Team spirit and chivalry are in disrepute and ordinary human intercourse in disarray.

The Cathechism reminds us gravely that God is neither male nor female but pure Spirit. This hasn't stopped a number of ladies from referring to Him as 'her'. Trying to visualize Him is a pointless exercise but while I can handle the notion of the Ancient of Days as an old person with white whiskers I cannot, cannot see Him in twin-set and pearls.

Fighting Talk

There are those who maintain that all conflict springs from religious sources: that differences of opinion arise between people who hold opposing views on what God said, and to whom He said it and precisely what He meant by it. They insist that if only religion were banished from the face of the earth then there would be no reason to argue and peace would reign. I don't know why they adhere so fiercely to this view because once you start prodding it it falls apart. Most religious wars, crusades, pogroms and jihads, while conducted under the banner of religion, are really an excuse to acquire spoils, riches and, most important of all, territory. Human, i.e. animal, nature is tribal and tribes need land. People tend to behave better when they confine themselves to what they can regard as their own patch. When they steal somebody else's land they begin by razing everything to the ground and then, when they've done that, they proceed to build their own house and look after it carefully: they are not so prone to litter it with beer cans and crisp bags and scrawl graffiti all over it.

You will doubtless be wondering why I'm going on in this tedious fashion about something so obvious. It is because of the robins. I don't believe robins have any religious convictions whatsoever and they are undoubtedly among the most ill-tempered and combative of God's creatures. They hate

147

people, they hate the cat and they hate each other. And they are unhinged on the subject of territory. They have been brawling on the balcony and in the lilac bush and the lower branches of the ash for days now, driving us all crazy for they have astonishingly loud and unmusical voices when their ire is raised. Tirelessly cross and endlessly vocal they chatter and scold from dawn to dusk and one ceases to wonder why they don't get along together and often murder each other. Out of the kindness of our hearts we have restrained Basil the cat from catching them and I sometimes begin to ask myself if we were not mistaken. As soon as anyone, human, feline or avian sets foot or wing in or over the pit we call the garden they start screaming abuse and are the worst of neighbours.

By contrast the dulcet-toned blackbird seems as gracious as a visiting opera star and I realize that we have previously appreciated him insufficiently. Even the sadly incontinent pigeons who earlier had a squat in the lime tree seem not so tiresome as the robins. Anyway they appear to have moved on and distance lends enchantment. The robins, who are probably aware that they have no absolute right to the lilac bush, behave like the more annoying New Age travellers, keeping up the cacophony long after the averagely psycho-logically secure citizen has grown fed up with it. They are xenophobic even within their own species. A man on the wireless said that not only did they quarrel with their nearest and dearest but they have regional accents and if a South Walian robin is introduced to a North London robin then all hell breaks loose. They will attack anything red under the impression that it is the front of another robin and will go on savaging it until it's all torn up.

I remember how my mother and I were flattered when a robin made a habit of walking into our cottage kitchen. Now I think he was only measuring the place up with a view to building his nest in it. The ones in the bush are determined to harass us until we move away. Then when they've got the place to themselves they'll spend their time posing for Christmas cards and everyone will say, 'Oh, how sweet.'

Equal in the Eyes of God

The other day Archbishop Carey gave utterance to the profound insight that racism was a bad thing. One wonders how many people suddenly sat bolt upright, astonished at this revelation, or how many National Front supporters paused in the process of having their heads tattooed to rethink their whole attitude to the subject. Mouthing doleful platitudes doesn't get us very far, but then nor does anything else. The race relations industry not infrequently engenders more resentment than it dissipates and I have great sympathy with my Nigerian friend who complained that she was perfectly capable of getting to the top of her profession by her own unaided efforts but nobody would ever believe that: they would all assume that she had reached the dizzying heights with the assistance of the liberal establishment, and if she hadn't been a black woman she'd still be making tea for the boss. I've known rich and well-born people who have suffered similarly. No matter how good they are at their jobs no one believes they really *deserve* their success. It is very annoying for them because what can they say without sounding vain and boastful? There has never been a satisfactory response to the remark, 'Oh it's all very well for you.' 'Equal opportunities' can sometimes mean something quite different. The competent detest being patronized but then, I suppose, so do we all. If a person is skilled at a particularly difficult task he is not grateful to those who seek to make the task simpler. It makes it look as though he'd been wasting his time. People who are good at sums or at spelling or baking biscuits do not want their accomplishments rendered foolproof. They would rather have a proper acknowledgement of their talent than be told there are easier new ways to go about it. Nor do many people wish to resemble in every respect all those by whom they are surrounded. The urge to homogeneity arises from misunderstanding and intolerance while a cheerful acceptance of diversity makes life more interesting. Last time we were in France we went round on various tourist routes and had to keep reminding ourselves where we were, for we could have been anywhere. There was none of that delightful sense of being in a strange and foreign country and almost everything we bought we could have bought at the delicatessen counter in our local supermarket. It was boring and boredom is not conducive to good behaviour: people who are bored carve rude messages in the upholstery of trains and get drunk. I moaned a lot about how different it had been in the old days and everyone got fed up with me. Travel used to be as fascinating as reading but now it's more like watching telly. There are few discoveries you can make for yourself. I suppose it's all down to the god Progress, and progress is the insult we pay not only to our ancestors but to all those who happen to think in different ways from our own Western mode. For a time it was *de rigueur* among right-thinking anthropologists to deny that before the intrusion of the 'civilized' world the Aztecs used to eat people. They did. They cooked them with chocolate and peppers and I expect they enjoyed them a lot. We may not approve of such behaviour but it is as offensive to pretend they didn't as to throw up our hands and denounce them as barbarians. There's a lot of chat in some circles about

151

re-discovering the truths in the old religions, but only when they've been dusted down and deodorized a bit in order to make them acceptable to current notions of propriety. If I was a pagan chewing on a person's femur I'd find it just as maddening as old-style colonialism. Patronizing people may not be as wrong as eating them but it comes close.

Breaking In, Breaking Out

I no longer know any burglars personally, which is strange when you consider how great has been the increase in crime in recent years. There are people who deny this and maintain that the media is making it all up and that matters are no worse than they ever were. Piffle – respond the rest of us. The son of a local shopkeeper was stabbed to death the other day and the terrible thing was that nobody was really surprised. We all know people who have been mugged, wounded, cheated or burgled and this is a recent development. Only a few years ago we often left our doors unlocked and felt no qualms about opening them to people who wanted to read the meter or sell us horse manure. Now we have a security gate and a phone to check on the identity of callers. There were thieves around certainly but we knew most of them and they usually stole things from the backs of lorries. Their families wouldn't let them remove the property of people they knew because it made for such an unpleasant atmosphere. Now the malefactors are mostly anonymous and not subject to the same restrictions: faceless and frightening.

At the moment I am regretting the scarcity of burglars among my close acquaintance because the alarm of a neighbour's car has been activated – almost certainly by a cat or just because it got its wires into a twist – and it has been cheeping for hours. If I knew a burglar or even a person who was given to Taking and Driving Away I would call him round and we would all help him push the damn thing in the canal. Its owners are all undoubtedly in the country enjoying a leisurely lunch to the sound of cows lowing and birds singing while we in town are being driven slowly mad. I have tried to tell myself that the noise is no more irritating than the sound of cicadas rubbing their back legs together or the croaking of mating bullfrogs but this is no consolation, since it isn't true. Natural noise can be annoying, particularly when nature's creatures, such as cocks, do it at the crack of dawn, but man-made noise is far worse.

I am growing more criminally inclined as the seconds go by. Many of the criminals I have known in my time have been amiable enough when not professionally engaged: good to their mothers (although not infrequently a little careless with regard to their wives who they often seemed to find a bit of a nuisance) and indulgent to their children. They used to disappear for months at a time and return with an unhealthy pallor, but seldom made a fuss about having been compelled to pay their debt to society. 'If you can't do time, don't do the crime,' they said. Prison was an occupational hazard.

Burglars were often quite candid about their chosen avocation, accepting the rules of the game and admitting when it was up – 'You got me bang to rights, guv', etc., but the murderers I have known have all been dreadful liars. This sheds an interesting light on human psychology. I would write a short dissertation on the matter if it wasn't for the noise of the car alarm. As it is I'm beginning to feel quite violent myself. I must remember not to murder the neighbour for it would undoubtedly have an adverse effect on my character. I might just go and break his windows. I fear these sentiments are unedifying, but there, the Church was made for sinners.

But Which Witch?

The other morning I heard on the radio a vicar suggesting that lady priests should be burned at the stake. It was not a witty remark and the vicar was clearly a few buns short of a vicarage tea party, nevertheless the next day there was a lady in the morning God-slot squawking away about the misogynistic implications of his utterance and reminding us of the horrors of Cromwell Street where the police were busily disinterring female remains. She seemed to consider this further evidence of a uniquely horrible conspiracy against women, leaving out of account the activities of such as Dennis Nilsen who focused his attention on men. And while it is true that many women were burned as witches, so is it true that many men were hanged, drawn and quartered – which can't have been much fun either. I am growing increasingly bored with the pretence that Western woman has been hideously oppressed until now while her menfolk enjoyed lives of blissful freedom and exercised their powers to keep the females in their place. Many years ago when the Chelsea Arts Club was exclusively male I was smuggled in by two gentlemen friends with my hair tucked into a man's cap and an army greatcoat concealing my contours (the pubs had closed, we were desperate for a drink and the club provided the nearest source of sustenance). I was aware only of an old tradition and did not get the impression that I was loathed because of my sex: *quite* the contrary. Women who complain that men have always denigrated them seem not to take into account the things that women say about men. I have, in my time, been shamed, after a good gossip with my chums about the iniquities and tiresome habits of our nearest and dearest, by the realization that our nearest and dearest did not habitually get together to air the deficiencies of their wives and girl-friends in the same way. My dear husband, who admittedly considers me uneducated, daffy and a touch untidy, does not fly to the telephone to describe my failings to his mates. Women, it now seems, dislike men rather more than men dislike women. Some of the things they say would make your hair curl and I know of all-female households where even a male canary is not permitted lest the pure atmosphere be contaminated by the level of testosterone.

I am also deeply weary of all the tosh that is talked about equality. We've got lady doctors and bank managers and lawyers, screech the egalitarians who seem incapable of following an argument. Why can't we have lady priests? Useless to say this is not a secular matter, for the issue is perceived in secular terms. The other day I remembered what my right arm is for: it's for holding a baby against my left shoulder so it can throw up on it. I was carrying the latest family member and feeling complete and useful in a way that I've missed since my youngest learned to cope with her own digestive processes. The perfect couple is a woman and a baby. You can keep the boardroom and the bank and the mobile telephone. I am perfectly happy with *Küche, Kinder, Kirche* – so long, that is, as I can have an occasional good gossip and a trip to the pub with a couple of the blokes to make a bit of a change.

Democratic Tyranny

I don't know why people suggest that Cardinal Ratzinger is much hated. Most of the Catholics I know see him as one of the few beacons of light in a heaving fog of trendy tripe. It is the progressives whom we regard askance. One of the elements in recent developments that we find strange is the disregard on the part of the progressive clergy of the wishes and inclinations of their parishioners. Despite all the talk of democracy, 'empowerment' of the laity, etc., we now seem to have a number of unrestrained and wilful priests who put their own foibles foremost, gaily ignoring both a large part of the congregation and what is laid down in Canon Law.

I have in my possession a heart-rending letter from some people to their bishop pleading for an answer to their very proper queries. Their church has been vandalized by their parish priest (at extravagant expense) and in other churches in the diocese altar girls are allowed. In the Instruction *Inaestimabile Donum*, issued by the Sacred Congregation for the Sacraments and Divine Worship 1980, it states categorically, 'Women however are not permitted to act as altar servers.' In his reply the bishop skates round this one and then loses his temper. He writes on a note of shrill indignation, astonished at being questioned and demanding an apology. He answers none of the queries, seems to care only about a spurious and cosmetic 'unity' within the parishes and boasts about his record. (It is said that there are more lapsed Catholics in his diocese than in any other in England and Wales.)

The people who wrote to him have gone to the trouble of studying the documents relating to those matters which concern them and have found themselves, to their anguish and frustration, summarily rebuffed by the very person to whom they turned for succour. I tried to telephone him, admittedly because I had a powerful desire to hit him with my handbag, and was fended off by another person of very few words. 'No, you can't talk to the bishop' was about the sum of them. 'Write a letter' was the suggestion. Clearly a pointless exercise (and how different from my experience in Ireland where all the clergy, even the highest, seem readily accessible).

'We have tried,' say his correspondents in their letter to me, 'as ordinary lay people who have suffered an injustice at the hands of the clergy, to pursue procedures as laid out in Canon Law (on the advice of the Canon Law Society of Great Britain and Ireland), but have hit a brick wall at every turn. The more we delve the more mysterious it becomes. The clergy have got away with too much for too long and they should not treat their own people with such contempt without the laity having some form of recourse. That recourse is laid out in Canon Law, but it would appear that Canon Law is not worth a carrot.'

I find the whole business frightening as well as infuriating. It is remarkable how those who claim to love their laity with unprecedented tenderness can turn so nasty. They appear indulgent to heresy and sin and seem only to dislike the faithful. What can the flock do when the shepherd prefers to spend his time chatting with the wolf?

Our People-pleasing Society

The other day, wholly unexpectedly, the Archbishop of Canterbury said something that on the face of it did not sound entirely idiotic. Critics have since pointed out that on closer investigation his observations do not hold water, but his remark about the 'ordinariness' of Britain struck a chord. The urge to make everything and everyone the same has rendered the place extraordinarily dull. People wearing the same clothes throng identical shopping malls, buying yet more similar clothes. It's hard to tell which city you're in unless you've gone by train and can consult your ticket to jog the memory.

Sometimes it's quite hard to tell whether you're in a Catholic or a Wee Free place of worship except that if the person out in front is leading the congregation in a rendition of 'All You Need Is Love', then in all probability he is one of the new breed of Catholic priests who sees his role as primarily that of people-pleaser.

Sentimentality on the part of the clergy does not inspire confidence in the people. Too many clergymen are adrift on a slimy slick of schmaltz, bleating away about how 'inclusive' are their attitudes; how loving and caring and sharing, how kind and supportive they are. But only question them, only hint that you do not accept their personal interpretation of religion and the jack boot is immediately apparent. As they free themselves from restraint their arrogance and stupidity are painfully obvious. Priests, bishops, archbishops, refuse to accept criticism of their antics, will not speak to people who are concerned about the influx of neo-pagan practices in their churches, who are appalled by the loss of reverence for the Eucharist or the destruction of church interiors and are frankly embarrassed by the sheer silliness of much that goes on in our places of worship. Worship in many cases has been put aside in the interests of what the innovators call 'active participation'. There is no place for meditative reverence when the feel-good factor is paramount. The sinister, truth-denying influence of New Ageism with its hysterical, orgiastic elements is increasingly prevalent, and a hideous, levelling sentimentality is creeping in everywhere.

The abuse of language is one of the signs. I read a piece about a woman who had 'shared' something over lunch. Wow, you think. She's handing round her jam butties. What a doll. But no. What she did was *tell* the assembled company about one of her feminist fantasies. She didn't *share* it with them. She *told* them. I can't remember what it was but I do seem to recall that it wasn't worth saying. This is frequently the case when the word 'sharing' is misused.

Religion is being simultaneously trivialized and politicized and when you try to ask an archbishop what the hell is going on his secretary hangs up the phone on you. I came across another woman talking about how she had once mischiev-ously asked her scripture teacher what circumcision meant (many respectable women like it to be known that they were naughty little things), as though this were highly original. Almost everyone I've ever known has tried that one on the scripture teacher – but when they grow up they try to forget about it. Dredging up such asininity is all part of the attempt to 'humanize' religion, to show that we're on everyday terms with the Almighty and have nothing to fear. But we have. We have a great deal to fear. The dismantling of our religion for a start.

Perishing Perishables

I'd forgotten what a nuisance fruit can be. We usually buy it and proceed to eat it, but over the festive season we buy it to look at, since it does have a decorative element. We tell ourselves that when we've looked at it for long enough we can transform it into fruit salad, thus exercising thrift as well as improving the health. Flowers are a nuisance too, especially the ones we buy in the market which begin to die the minute you put them in the vase. However, there is no further use for dead flowers unless you have a compost heap, and even then they look pitiful and faintly reproachful, as though it was your fault they'd been ripped from their native heath, or wherever they came from, only to end up with the potato peelings, tea bags and egg shells. Left-over fruit evokes a different guilt, the sort that arises from the careless frittering away of money and the waste of good food. A pineapple sat glaring at us for weeks, the grapes shrivelled into raisins before our eyes, the apples wrinkled, the tangerines shrank, and every time we thought of fruit salad somebody would say they didn't fancy it today and could we not have the ice-cream or the chocolate cake instead. In the end and in the nick of time I persuaded a family member to prepare the pineapple: this is a peculiarly exasperating and painful task since the thing has unexpected spikes and prickles and clings to its skin, unlike the better designed, more user-friendly grapefruit, orange or banana. It is the fruity equivalent of those cartons which refuse to relinquish their contents and break the fingernails: sometimes you are forced into wrenching at them with your teeth, which gives you an appearance at once ineffectual and demented. The pineapple also makes a lot of mess with leaves and rind, gritty bits and juice all spilling over the board and into the bowl. I hate them and so, it seems, does everyone else, for it has now sat in the fridge for a day and a night while people go on eating the ice-cream and the chocolate cake. We have discarded the more hopelessly festering grapes, but left a few in case anyone fancies them. The remaining mandarins are flanking a solitary grapefruit and the overall effect is no longer particularly decorative but rather sad, reminding me of the Four Last Things and the fact that the party's over.

The cat can always eat the rest of the turkey but unless you keep a fruit-bat as a pet the peeled pineapple and the spurned oranges are your own responsibility.

Then we come to the nuts. The larger, more succulent ones have been all eaten up and there remain the small unwanted ones, poor rejected spinsters and bachelors like those chocolates that always get left in the box – the hard ones with the unpleasing centres. We have also mislaid the nutcracker and I have evolved a method of cracking brazils under a table leg which necessitates careful judgement and muscular control followed by a session with the dustpan and brush. But the final challenge remains. The coconut. This uncouth object has the air of daring us to tackle it. It looks untidy and dangerous and well able to stand up for itself. I'm waiting for the menfolk to assemble before declaring war on it. Killing a coconut is no job for a lady. Far too much nuisance.

Circus Maximus

I watched *Ben Hur* the other day. Well, most of it. The chariot race makes me giddy and I have heard that horses were killed and maimed during the course of this scene. It seems probable that several human beings also suffered laceration and bruising, since it is intensely energetic, but one reasons that they knew what they were in for and getting well paid. My sympathies here lie with the horses. I am reminded of the story of the child who kept making his parents take him to see a statue of Gordon of Khartoum atop his camel. They were pleased with the kiddie's patriotic instincts and his recognition of a national hero until one day he asked, 'Daddy, who's that man sitting on Gordon?' Animals can often seem to hold more appeal than our own species. Throughout the film whenever Charlton Heston (I think it was he) appeared I found myself musing – that man is in the grip of some powerful emotion. The sinews of his neck stood out, the sweat sprang from his forehead and he clenched his jaw. He did so much of it it must have been almost more tiring than the race. His mother and sister, on the other hand, reacted with remarkable calm to the traumas to which they had been subjected. Today someone would have insisted, at the very least, that they should undergo counselling. When some miserable burglar pinched our TV and video and a number of trifles that were lying round, we received a letter offering us this service. I was extremely annoyed by the robbery and I hope the burglar swallows his teeth, but I didn't feel the need of therapy.

It's a funny old world, both as represented in Biblical epic and every day on our streets. The ancient Romans were a nasty lot but then so are many of our contemporaries: we seem not to learn the lessons of history, even with the help of films like *Ben Hur*. I find it strange that the authorities should wish to make a fuss of me because my TV got nicked while permitting people in real need of help to sleep in doorways and endanger their lives. Our leaders appear to have a tenuous grasp of reality, imagining that human nature has somehow changed radically in recent times and the community – whatever they think they mean by that – is ready and eager to accept the ill and the anti-social in its midst in a spirit of Christian charity. This charity doubtless exists in groups here and there but unfortunately is not widespread. Our local policeman, whom I much prefer to Ben Hur, has a terrible time trying to dissuade the homeless from mugging each other, let alone the wealthy; while the reaction of much of the citizenry to the unkempt and forlorn is not dissimilar from that of the cast of the above epic who gathered their garments about them and threw stones at the lepers.

Giving Up the Habit

I do miss nuns: real, proper, copper-bottomed, kosher nuns clad in full habit with the accompanying rattle of rosary beads. There used to be a convent at the top of our road and every day we would hear the Angelus ringing above the traffic noise. There seemed to be hundreds of nuns, resident and visiting, sweeping round in a flourish of skirt and veil. My children went there for scripture lessons and I used to go to the quiet chapel, leaving the sisters to cope with them for a while. Very restful it was (until the children realized the potential of the slippery corridors, which made it difficult for me to extract them with dignity). There was a pleasant garden and once a year there would be a fête to which all the neighbours went, regardless of their religious affiliations. Most of them are committed atheists but there was always a good display of junk in the jumble sale and everyone likes to find treasure in the midst of dross. The teas were very good too. There used to be a real feeling of community in that convent garden on a summer Saturday afternoon. It wasn't thought of as that then of course: no one talked about the concept of community until the reality of it was lost. Now the nuns have gone, the building has changed hands often and appears to be changing hands again, and there's nowhere so convenient for the neighbours to meet so we don't, except by chance in the supermarket. The nuns have all dispersed or died. A few, I believe, live in a little house somewhere. I saw one or two for a while after the disaster: they looked cold and ugly and ordinary in ill-cut clothes and anoraks, with their hair sticking out under their scarves, and had lost all the confidence which had somehow been implicit in their appearance, in their distinctive habit. They reminded me of bathers who have had their garments stolen and must needs walk home inadequately clad: they had the same slightly rueful, slightly apologetic air.

It is customary at present for women who went to convent school in the forties and fifties to claim that they were given a really tough time and had to obey a lot of rules; no talking in class, no running in the corridors, no kissing boys in the vicinity of the school, etc. The fact is that anyone who went to practically any school pre-sixties would have met the same entirely sensible attitudes. The rules of my girls-only secular grammar school would strike the child of today as being medieval, but they saved a lot of time and trouble. You knew where you were. Now nobody seems to know where anybody is – especially in inner-city schools.

I'm thinking about nuns at present because some friends just sent me a framed quotation written out by the Carmelite Mother Michael who I knew in the old days when she and her fellow nuns were building their own convent chapel; sleeves rolled up, skirts kilted as they pushed wheelbarrows up ramps and laid bricks. They did not quite fit into the caricature image of the repressed religious which today's liberal likes to evoke, but were cheerful, practical women with a strength and holiness lacking in certain sisters (who shall be nameless) whom I have come across recently and who put a great strain on one's Christian charity. Mother Michael's message reads, 'Sing with unwearied strength, very loud, with a great voice, sweetly far and near.' It makes a welcome change from the weasel words, the oily platitudes, the saccharine advice offered to us by so many of our leaders both secular and religious. Oh how I miss nuns.

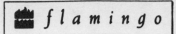

flamingo

Flamingo is a quality imprint publishing both fiction and non fiction. Below are some recent titles.

Fiction

☐ No Other Life *Brian Moore* £5.99
☐ The Kitchen God's Wife *Amy Tan* £4.99
☐ A Thousand Acres *Jane Smiley* £5.99
☐ A Yellow Raft in Blue Water *Michael Dorris* £5.99
☐ Tess *Emma Tennant* £5.99
☐ Pepper *Tristan Hawkins* £5.99
☐ Dreaming in Cuban *Cristina Garcia* £5.99
☐ Happenstance *Carol Shields* £5.99
☐ Blood Sugar *Suzannah Dunn* £5.99
☐ Postcards *E. Annie Proulx* £5.99

Non-fiction

☐ The Gates of Paradise *Alberto Manguel* £9.99
☐ Sentimental Journeys *Joan Didion* £5.99
☐ Epstein *Stephen Gardiner* £8.99
☐ Love, Love and Love *Sandra Bernhard* £5.99
☐ City of Djinns *William Dalrymple* £5.99
☐ Dame Edna Everage *John Lahr* £5.99
☐ Tolstoy's Diaries *R. F. Christian* £7.99
☐ Wild Swans *Jung Chang* £7.99

You can buy Flamingo paperbacks at your local bookshop or newsagent. Or you can order them from HarperCollins Mail Order, Dept. 8. HarperCollins*Publishers*, Westerhill Road, Bishopbriggs, Glasgow G64 2QT. Please enclose a cheque or postal order, to the order of the cover price plus add £1.00 for the first and 25p for additional books ordered within the UK.

NAME (Block letters)_____

ADDRESS_____

_____